Centre for Educational Research and Innovation (CERI)

IN-SERVICE EDUCATION AND TRAINING OF TEACHERS

A condition for educational change

ORGANISATION FOR ECONOMIC CO-OPERATION AND DEVELOPMENT

The Organisation for Economic Co-operation and Development (OECD) was set up under a Convention signed in Paris on 14th December 1960, which provides that the OECD shall promote policies designed:
- to achieve the highest sustainable economic growth and employment and a rising standard of living in Member countries, while maintaining financial stability, and thus to contribute to the development of the world economy;
- to contribute to sound economic expansion in Member as well as non-member countries in the process of economic development;
- to contribute to the expansion of world trade on a multilateral, non-discriminatory basis in accordance with international obligations.

The Members of OECD are Australia, Austria, Belgium, Canada, Denmark, Finland, France, the Federal Republic of Germany, Greece, Iceland, Ireland, Italy, Japan, Luxembourg, the Netherlands, New Zealand, Norway, Portugal, Spain, Sweden, Switzerland, Turkey, the United Kingdom and the United States.

The Centre for Educational Research and Innovation was created in June 1968 by the Council of the Organisation for Economic Co-operation and Development for an initial period of three years, with the help of grants from the Ford Foundation and the Royal Dutch Shell Group of Companies. In May 1971, the Council decided that the Centre should continue its work for a period of five years as from 1st January 1972. In July 1976 it extended this mandate for the following five years, 1977-82.

The main objectives of the Centre are as follows:
- *to promote and support the development of research activities in education and undertake such research activities where appropriate;*
- *to promote and support pilot experiments with a view to introducing and testing innovations in the educational system;*
- *to promote the development of co-operation between Member countries in the field of educational research and innovation.*

The Centre functions within the Organisation for Economic Co-operation and Development in accordance with the decisions of the Council of the Organisation, under the authority of the Secretary-General. It is supervised by a Governing Board composed of one national expert in its field of competence from each of the countries participating in its programme of work.

Publié en français sous le titre :

LA FORMATION EN COURS DE SERVICE
DES ENSEIGNANTS
Condition du changement à l'école

© OECD, 1982
Application for permission to reproduce or translate all or part of this publication should be made to:
Director of Information, OECD
2, rue André-Pascal, 75775 PARIS CEDEX 16, France.

CONTENTS

Preface 5
    I. Introduction: The Evolution of the Project 9
   II. The Importance and Scope of INSET 10
  III. Teachers' Characteristics and INSET Needs 14
   IV. The Role of the School 20
    V. Training the Trainers 31
   VI. Costs, Finances and Resources 38
  VII. Evaluation: Techniques and Policies 47
 VIII. Effective INSET 53
   IX. Main Conclusions and their Implications for Policy and Research 58
    X. A Framework for the Development of New Policies 76
   XI. Bibliography 79

Chart: Structure and Content of the "Inset Project" 1975-80 7

Also available

INNOVATION IN IN-SERVICE EDUCATION AND TRAINING OF TEACHERS. PRACTICE AND THEORY (August 1978)
(96 78 04 1) ISBN 92-64-11809-8   64 pages   £1.70   US$3.50   F14.00

Prices charged at the OECD Publications Office.

THE OECD CATALOGUE OF PUBLICATIONS and supplements will be sent free of charge on request addressed either to OECD Publications Office, 2, rue André-Pascal, 75775 PARIS CEDEX 16, or to the OECD Sales Agent in your country.

PREFACE

This publication marks the successful termination of a six-year investigatory project conducted by the Centre for Educational Research and Innovation with financial aid from the United States' National Institute of Education.

The project began in response to the widely felt need for sound programming of in-service education and training to equip teachers with new techniques, methods and attitudes corresponding with their changing roles and tasks. It concluded with the finding, backed by a wealth of specialist studies in many Member countries, that in the near future national education systems will have to give priority to in-service training of education personnel for a number of reasons, of which these four are the most compelling:

- schools must be capable at all times of responding in various ways to the varied needs of their pupils and of society;
- the functions, attitudes and qualifications of school personnel will therefore continue to play a fundamental role in the national life;
- in view of the decreasing recruitment, there is still a need to maintain the internal dynamism of the teaching profession;
- the increasing complexity of the problems that confront each individual school and which it must endeavour to solve under conditions of optimum freedom of action implies that, more than hitherto, training activities should centre on the school and take an increasingly collaborative form, implying that related solid support structures need to be set up by the responsible authorities.

The six years of work consisted of two phases. The first achieved a broad dissemination of national practices and experience to enable comparative analyses on an international scale. This entailed the preparation of a series of national monographs covering ten countries and their consideration at an international seminar in Philadelphia in 1976 at which innovative practices of INSET were reviewed in an attempt to place them within a conceptual framework. A synthesis of the results of the survey of country experience and of this seminar were published as an interim report (<u>Innovation in In-service Education and Training of Teachers: Practice and Theory</u>).

This first phase of informative gathering, analysis and international assessment enabled the identification of six subject areas where, in particular, the results of the investigation could be generally applied or adapted to actual national conditions. These were: The Contribution of Adult Learning Theories and Practices to INSET; The Role of the School; Evaluation; New INSET Materials; The Role of Training Teachers; The Cost and Efficient Utilisation of INSET Resources. It is these that have provided the substance of phase two of the INSET programme, CERI's full range of experimental methods, multinational co-operation, co-development activities and specialist enquiry being deployed in their pursuit. Progress has been reviewed periodically in seminars and workshops in various of the Member countries concerned. The structure and range of the programme are illustrated in the accompanying chart.

The culmination of this phase, and hence of the project, was an intergovernmental conference held in Paris on 29th September-1st October 1980 with an attendance of over 80 - national delegates, observers from bodies professionally concerned and subject specialists. This brought together the results of all the component activities for review and assessment. The Conference also agreed on a number of precepts that together constitute a framework within which policies for in-service education and training of teachers and strategies for educational change can be realistically debated or, indeed, conceived. These (see Section X) should be of considerable interest to national planning authorities for social matters and education.

The report that follows has been prepared by Dr. R. Bolam of the University of Bristol, United Kingdom, as a synthesis of all the studies and activity reports contributed to the final phase of the project. Its purpose is to bring within a single conspectus the results of experiments, lessons learned or unprofitable approaches gleaned from a very wide field. Those responsible for policy or for practice at national or local levels may thus extract from the experience of colleagues abroad ideas and practices that, suitably adapted, can help to improve INSET in their own countries.

J.R. Gass,
Director,
Centre for Educational
Research and Innovation

STRUCTURE AND CONTENT OF THE «INSET PROJECT», 1975-1980

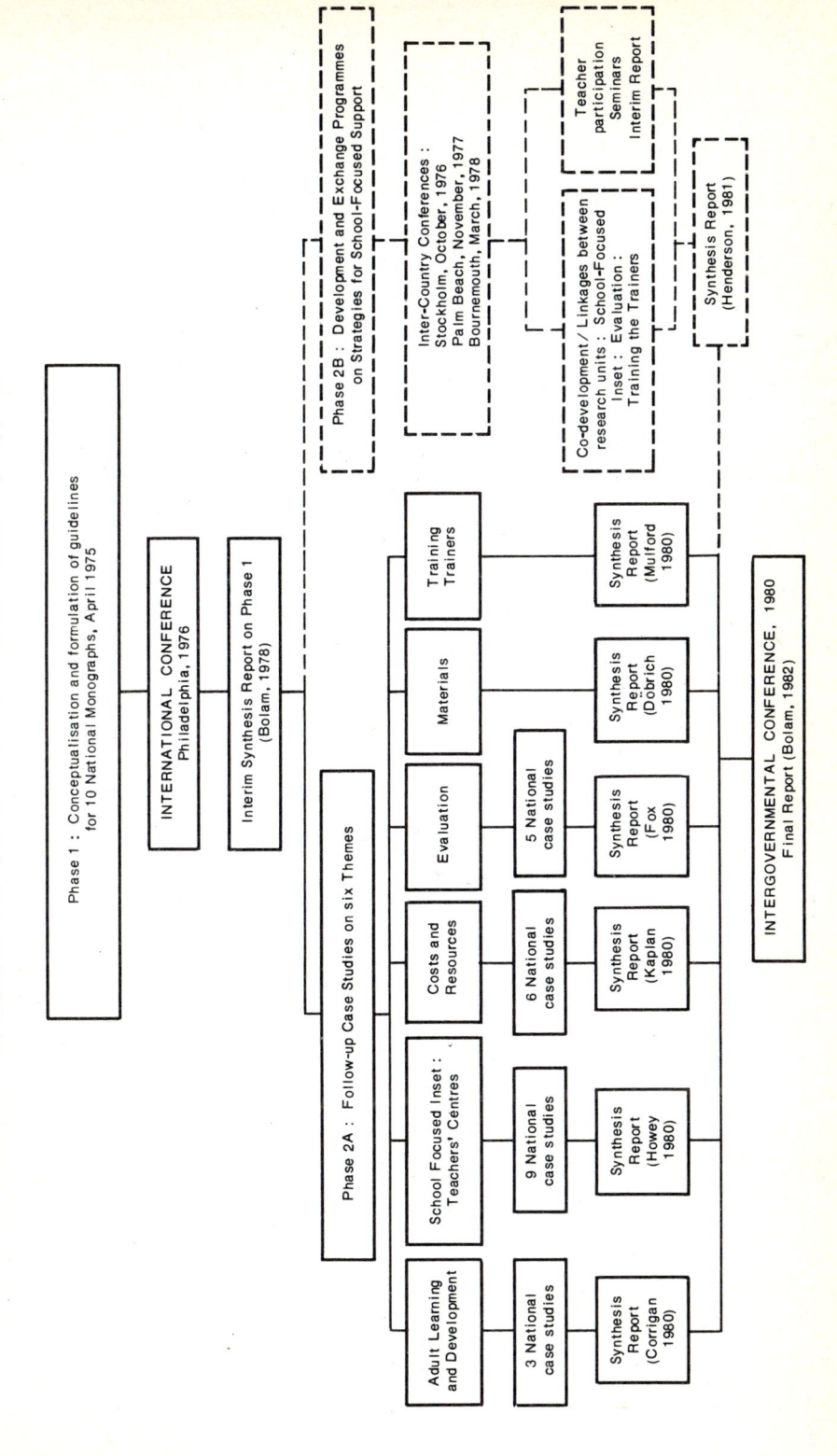

```
Phase 1 : Conceptualisation and formulation of guidelines
for 10 National Monographs, April 1975
          │
          ▼
INTERNATIONAL CONFERENCE
Philadelphia, 1976
          │
          ▼
Interim Synthesis Report on Phase 1
(Bolam, 1978)
          │
          ▼
Phase 2A : Follow-up Case Studies on six Themes
          │
┌─────────┬─────────────┬──────────┬──────────┬──────────┬──────────┐
│         │             │          │          │          │          │
Adult     School        Costs      Evaluation  Materials  Training
Learning  Focused       and                               Trainers
and       Inset :       Resources
Development Teachers'
          Centres
│         │             │          │          │          │
3 National 9 National   6 National 5 National
case       case         case       case
studies    studies      studies    studies
│         │             │          │          │          │
Synthesis Synthesis     Synthesis  Synthesis  Synthesis  Synthesis
Report    Report        Report     Report     Report     Report
(Corrigan (Howey        (Kaplan    (Fox       (Döbrich   (Mulford
1980)     1980)         1980)      1980)      1980)      1980)
```

Phase 2B : Development and Exchange Programmes on Strategies for School-Focused Support

Inter-Country Conferences :
Stockholm, October, 1976
Palm Beach, November, 1977
Bournemouth, March, 1978

Co-development / Linkages between research units : School-Focused Inset : Evaluation : Training the Trainers

Teacher participation Seminars Interim Report

Synthesis Report (Henderson, 1981)

INTERGOVERNMENTAL CONFERENCE, 1980
Final Report (Bolam, 1982)

I. INTRODUCTION

This final report is designed to synthesise the outcomes of a lengthy and complex project, to consider these in the context of some related research findings and of wider developments in education and, finally, to highlight certain policy implications. In selecting ideas and findints for this synthesis the writer has naturally drawn most largely on the distinguished professional documentation from many countries with which the project has been supplied. These studies and reports (more than thirty in number) are, in a sense, "occasional papers" and it is not the intention to publish them formally. The author trusts, however, that in what follows he has done them justice - within, of course, the limits set on one whose task is that of synthesis. All the contributors are credited by name and title in the Bibliography.

The project itself has been introduced and outlined in the foregoing Preface and its scope may be taken in with a glance at the accompanying chart. As will be seen, Phase 1 was concluded with the publication of an Interim Report (11)*. Phase 2, with which we are principally concerned here, was a two-branched undertaking, culminating in an Intergovernmental Conference in 1980. The first branch consisted of studies of six priority areas:

   i) the contribution of adult learning theories and practices to INSET (national case-studies);
  ii) the role of the school in INSET (national case-studies);
 iii) the evaluation of INSET (national case-studies);
  iv) new INSET materials;
   v) role and training of teacher trainers;
  vi) INSET financing and resources (national case-studies).

For the second branch of Phase 2 (which was mainly funded by the participating countries) a series of co-development activities, in the form of nationally sponsored conferences, seminars and site visits for practitioners and researchers were organised. These will continue on a group and bilateral basis as long as the participants consider them worthwhile.

---

*Figures between brackets refer to the Bibliography at the end of this volume.

9

II. THE IMPORTANCE AND SCOPE OF INSET

The Interim Report (11) concluded that there were three main reasons for the recent growth in commitment of national governments to INSET. First, it was inherently important that teachers, of all people, should continue with their personal and professional education; second, the rapid, extensive and fundamental nature of present-day change - technological, economic, cultural, social, political - made it imperative for the education system in general and teachers in particular to review and modify teaching methods and curricula; third, for widely prevalent demographic reasons, the demand for new teachers was dropping sharply and the INSET needs of a stable teaching force thereby became especially important.

The same report (p. 46) showed also that there was broad agreement in Member countries that INSET could and should make an important contribution to the resolution of problems associated with several contemporary, major task areas in education:

a) the curricular problems associated with the extension of compulsory schooling, especially the needs of the 13-16 age group;
b) the needs of special school populations, such as immigrant groups, multi-ethnic communities and disadvantaged rural communities;
c) the needs associated with particular subjects, notably science and mathematics, and student groups, notably those with special educational needs (i.e. variants on the mainstreaming problem);
d) the new demands on teachers caused by the radically changing nature of school-community relationships, e.g.

    - relations between education and working life;
    - renewed community demands for accountability related to educational standards and assessment;

e) the curricular and organisational consequences of declining enrolments;

f) the strategic need to provide adequate INSET for those with internal school management responsibilities.

There was, and continues to be, less agreement about the precise nature of INSET. In the present report it is understood as those education and training activities engaged in by primary and secondary school teachers and principals, following their initial professional certification, and intended mainly or exclusively to improve their professional knowledge, skills and attitudes in order that they can educate children more effectively. This definition will not meet with complete agreement either within or between Member countries, but it does reflect the main purposes for which the term has actually been used in most of the project documentation.

The point can perhaps be made more clearly by analysing a range of INSET purposes in the context of continuing education and the demands of system and individual needs. The generic term "continuing education" (or recurrent, adult, lifelong education or l'éducation permanente) is generally thought to embrace two broad components – personal education and vocational training. We may accordingly distinguish between five main purposes of continuing education for teachers:

1. Improving the job performance skills of the whole school staff or of groups of staff (e.g. a school-focused INSET programme).
2. Improving the job performance skills of an individual teacher (e.g. an induction programme for a beginning teacher).
3. Extending the experience of an individual teacher for career development or promotion purposes (e.g. a leadership training course).
4. Developing the professional knowledge and understanding of an individual teacher (e.g. a Master's degree in educational studies).
5. Extending the personal or general education of an individual (e.g. a Master's degree course not in education or a subject related to teaching).

A widely recognised problem in all organisations is that of reconciling the potential conflict between meeting the requirements and goals of the organisational system and of satisfying the needs for self-fulfilment of the individual member of an organisation. Adapting a diagram from Getzels and Guba (72), we can relate this problem to the five purposes of continuing education for teachers.

In this diagram Purpose 1 is seen as most likely to satisfy the requirements of the system for meeting its goals and least likely to meet the needs of individuals for self-fulfilment, while the reverse is the case with

Diagram 1   **SYSTEM AND INDIVIDUAL NEED FACTORS AND THE PURPOSES OF CONTINUING EDUCATION**

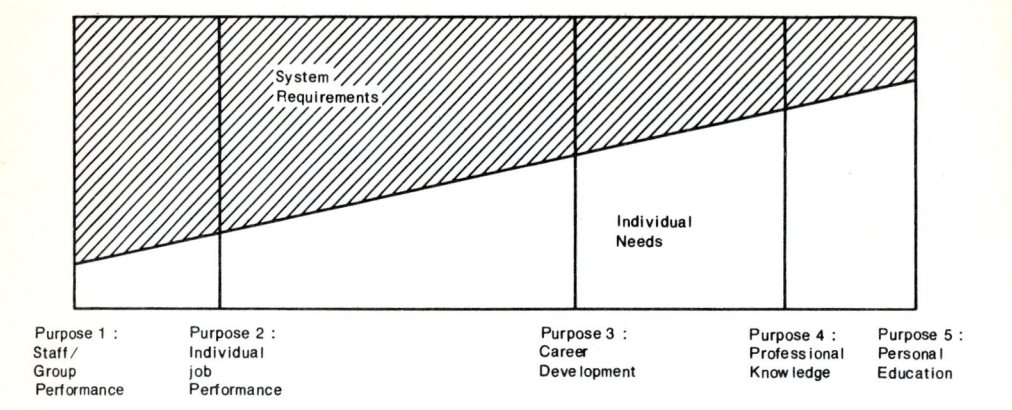

| Purpose 1: Staff/ Group Performance | Purpose 2: Individual job Performance | Purpose 3: Career Development | Purpose 4: Professional Knowledge | Purpose 5: Personal Education |

Purpose 5. It is, of course, recognised that any one INSET course may have several purposes but the diagram does illustrate Henderson's point made in "The Concept of School-Focused In-service Education and Training" (81) that a useful distinction can be made between the main and incidental purposes and outcomes of an INSET activity.

These issues were discussed in the submission by the teachers' representatives to the Intergovernmental Conference (119):

> "Whereas INSET is primarily based on utilitarian concerns, in particular the adaptation and extension of teaching techniques, a teacher's permanent education is designed more to encourage his desire for personal achievement and to fulfil his personal aspirations. It meets the need for each individual person constantly to be renewing the basic elements of his personal culture, in a changing world where values are changing all the time. In fact, the concept of permanent education cannot be opposed to that of in-service training; on the contrary, permanent education is one of the essential elements of such training, the one that concerns the teacher's professional life. One could even say that permanent education, seen in this light, should bring into closer relationship strictly cultural values and professional values, work and leisure; aspects of a person's life that the world of today has contributed to fragment and even to bring into opposition."

A similar position was adopted in the "James Report" (61), while alternative definitions and some of their implications are considered in at least two project reports, Marklund and Eklund's on Sweden (7) and Fox's Synthesis Report on Evaluation (30).

The indications from the reports and case studies produced during the project are that personal education (Purpose 5) is generally seen as an incidental aim and outcome of INSET by both teachers and employers; that teachers and, particularly, employers and principals are keen on Purposes 1 and 2; that certain teachers are keen on INSET for career development (Purpose 3); that universities and professional associations support the provision of professional knowledge for understanding (Purpose 4) and personal education (Purpose 5); and that teachers may attend INSET for professional knowledge (Purpose 4) partly in the hope that it will help them achieve promotion (Purpose 3).

Several general concluding points are worth making. First, that in practice, INSET is concerned with Purposes 1 and 2 in all Member countries, with Purposes 3 and 4 in many Member countries and with Purpose 5 in a few Member countries. Second, that the preference of employing authorities for Purposes 1 and 2 is most evident when they are required to release teachers to attend INSET courses. Third, that INSET needs are complex and likely to be given different priority by the various interested parties; hence the need for appropriate machinery to negotiate and agree upon them.

III. TEACHERS' CHARACTERISTICS AND INSET NEEDS

At an early stage in the project it was recognised that a fresh look at the characteristics and needs of teachers as adult learners was needed if their role in INSET was to be better understood, and one of the Phase 2 activities dealt specifically with this theme.

The French contribution here, by Gilles Ferry (14), relates teacher needs directly to the wider question of adult and continuing education. Since adulthood can be defined in terms of age and development which follows childhood and adolescence, Ferry concludes that a psychologically-oriented theory of adult education is needed. However, since adulthood can also be defined as a status which is dependent upon socio-economic factors, then a sociologically-oriented theory is also needed.

Ferry goes on to argue that, necessary as these psychological and sociological theories are, the most important feature of effective adult education is the opportunity for the "trainees" to participate in decisions about the design, implementation and evaluation of the programme. He also notes that the educational needs of a professional demand more than the learning of techniques and methods: continuing education for a profession (or, one might add, a semi-profession) embraces its whole institutional continuum, with its own system of standards, network of relations, and culture.

The theme of the teacher as a working adult is also taken up in a British contribution. Chambers (12) stresses the importance of the ways in which a teacher views and values himself or herself in in-school and private situations. Central as work is to most teachers' lives, at least four other focal interests occupy an individual's thought and time: the self, family, leisure and community. In order to illustrate their impact upon INSET, Chambers outlines two case studies of hypothetical teachers. The second study is of a female 24-year-old history honours graduate from a sheltered religious home background. She has been plunged into a "down-town" secondary comprehensive school to teach history and some religious education, mainly to third, fourth and fifth year mixed classes of "hardies". Her post-graduate

certificate of education training has "sprayed" her
lightly with theoretical concepts from Piaget, Bruner and
Vigotsky but that theoretical background, allied to her
twelve weeks' teaching practice in an open-access sixth-
form secondary college of self-selected pupils, has not
been greatly relevant (or developmental) in enabling her
to acquire the necessary "coping skills" for the work she
now has to face daily.

Chambers continues that the postulate would lead one
to suppose that this teacher's "vocational-self" construct
could be: "I am a total and abysmal failure" and that
this arose from a perceived rejection of everything she
had to offer by the pupils, reinforced by the all-too-
apparent attitudes of her long-suffering colleagues whose
patience was wearing thin at their failure to assist her
in gaining class-control, and compounded still further by
her spending the greater part of her private, out-of-
school time alone in a two-room, self-contained flat.
However, she has recently become engaged and, as a result,
her range of communication skills has extended beyond a
preoccupation with her own failures. She is now, therefore, better able to incorporate other people's needs,
ideas and values - including those of the pupils - into
her own "system" and her teaching ability is improving
slightly as a consequence. Because she is now less in
need of rewarding feedback she is becoming less flexible
and more authoritarian. From needing "salvation",
Chambers suggests that she could now be motivated to attend
an INSET course by the need for "reorientation" or, even,
"self-evaluation" if she is, by now, not too much at risk.

Writing from an American viewpoint, Corrigan,
Haberman and Howey (13) argue that INSET has neither been
regarded as adult education nor used theories of adult
learning because learning theories have been developed in
relation to animals and children and because, in any case,
INSET has some important, distinctive features. They
derive seven theoretical orientations from the literature
on adult education. First, psychometric research on
adults has found mainly negative correlations between age
and tests of intelligence, achievement, memory and
creativity. On the other hand, a second theoretical
orientation stresses the positive potential of the ageing
process because older people have accumulated more knowledge and experience; however, there are few research
data to support this approach. Mastery learning theory
generates propositions about motivation, feedback,
readiness, etc. which, though sometimes contradictory,
not of equal importance and not equally research-based,
appear to have direct relevance to adult learning.
Personal development theory contends that adult development is a continuation of early (i.e. child) internal
development and involves a series of stages or phases in
which different life tasks and therefore needs arise.
Organisation theory indicates that the situational

pressures upon individuals have to be taken into account, and changed, if meaningful learning is to occur. Finally, <u>group learning theory</u> stresses the significant influence of peer groups on individual learning.

The implications of each theoretical orientation are then explored by applying them to INSET. For example, the writers suggest that some form of compensatory education would be an appropriate way of responding to older students who were thought to require extra help because of the ageing-negative process; an approach based on a group learning orientation might use work groups and teams as the basic learning group. The value of this study probably lies mainly in the fact that it provides the first "map" of a hitherto unexplored aspect of INSET which should prove especially useful for research purposes.

What of the value of the American, British and French studies of adult learning for INSET programme designers and trainers? They undoubtedly act as sensitisers to the importance of the various characteristics of teachers as adult learners and to new ways of approaching the adult learning process. However, as an example, a careful reading of the US contribution suggests that although the seven theoretical orientations are sometimes mutually supportive they are not necessarily compatible and may even be mutually contradictory. Furthermore, in most real-life INSET programme settings the students are of different ages, sexes and from different personal and school circumstances and so the trainer's problems are compounded.

However, although the case studies do not offer many examples of good, feasible practice based directly upon theories of adult learning, those that are described are of considerable relevance and value to practitioners. For instance, Ferry (14) describes the changes that have occurred over a twelve-year period in France in the design of a long course for specialist educators. Over this time, he says, the formula has practically been reversed: occupational training, defined and controlled by the institution, has given way to personal training which the trainee designs and implements with the resources put at his disposal. The idea of training educators in accordance with the demands of the institution has changed to one of creating conditions in which the educators have an opportunity to train themselves.

Writing from the United Kingdom, Elliott (67) sets out to answer the question "How do teachers learn?" arguing:

> "... that intelligent practice - for example, knowing how to perform educational activities like teaching, curriculum development, and evaluation - cannot directly spring from a knowledge of theoretical principles about

practice, since these principles themselves derive from the analysis of practice. They are abstractions from the practical knowledge embodied in concrete performances. This argument has three important implications. First, practical knowledge cannot be reduced to the conscious application of principles, and this means the latter cannot explain how people learn to acquire and develop their practical skills. Secondly, genuine theoretical statements about practice cannot be understood a priori. One does not first understand a theoretical principle about education and then apply it in an analysis of practice. The understanding emerges from the analysis. Thirdly, theories about concrete practices, rather than their generalisable features, cannot be formal theories located within an academic discipline. Unlike the latter they are bound to a particular substantive context."

Elliott then goes on to describe in detail his attempts to apply these ideas to an advanced course in curriculum studies for experienced teachers.

Surveys of teachers' INSET needs are more familiar and have been carried out in many countries at all system levels - national, state, local authority and school. These provide information about self-reported needs in relation, for instance, to the teaching of particular subjects and to the management of schools. Other surveys and research projects have focused on teachers' needs at different career stages.

For example, a series of research and development studies have been carried out into the induction and training needs of beginning teachers in England and Wales (55). These have led to the broad conclusion that the overwhelming concern of most probationers is with the practicalities of their own teaching situation and that practical relevance is the principal yardstick by which they will judge an induction programme.

The project also led to the formulation of a rationale which can best be understood within the chronology of the school year. The probationers' needs are said to begin at the time of appointment. Following this, orientation to the routines and procedures of the school and LEA can take place during a pre-service visit or during the first days and weeks of the autumn term. The adaptation period is one in which the probationer is coming to terms with and reconciling the, frequently conflicting, demands of the school, the pupils, his own inclinations and the advice given to him in initial training: in short, he is formulating his own teaching style in a particular context. Towards the end of the autumn term, most LEAs ask the head to complete a progress assessment form so that probationers at risk can be identified. From about Christmas onwards, the majority of probationers have settled in and are ready for more sustained training activities to meet their professional development needs. The final assessment form is usually completed towards the end of the summer term and can be used to stimulate an overview both of the past year's experience and of career and in-service education and training opportunities during the second year and beyond. The six stages were not seen as sequential or developmental; rather they were offered as a tentative mapping device for those responsible for helping beginning teachers.

The work of Fuller in the United States (71) provides an alternative perspective on developmental needs in relation to the job. The most recent formulation offers a model based upon measures of teachers' stages of concern:

    I. Early phase   0 Concerns about self (non-teaching concerns)

   II. Middle phase   1 Concerns about professional expectations and acceptance
                             2 Concerns about one's own adequacy: subject matter and class control
                             3 Concerns about relationships with pupils

  III. Late phase   4 Concerns about pupils' learning what is taught
                             5 Concerns about pupils' learning what they need
                             6 Concerns about one's own (teacher's) contributions to pupil change.

(Adapted from Fuller by Feiman-Nemser and Floden)(69).

Policy makers, teacher educators and teachers' associations have often concentrated on the career needs of teachers. For example, an attempt was made by a national committee for INSET in England and Wales to devise an INSET needs framework based upon the likely career patterns of teachers. The concept of a career profile included the following key stages:

- the induction year;
- a consolidation period of four to six years during which teachers would attend short, specific courses;
- a reorientation period, after six to eight years experience, which could involve a secondment for a one term course and a change in career development;

- a period of further studies, in advanced seminars, to develop specialist expertise;
- at about mid-career, after about twelve to fifteen years, some teachers would benefit from advanced studies programmes of one year or more in length, possibly to equip them for leadership roles;
- after mid-career, a minority would need preparation for top management roles while the majority would need regular opportunities for refreshment.

As with the examples cited earlier in this section, it is important to question the status and usefulness of these studies. Their main value is probably as tools for deepening our understanding but, like all typologies and models, they oversimplify in order to achieve this. Thus, although the induction year stages provide an analytic tool which has proved useful during a research and development phase, no individual probationer's experience is likely to fit neatly into these stages. Similarly, no individual teacher is likely to move in a straightforward linear fashion through Fuller's stages of concern which, in any case, do not deal with the teacher's concerns about herself or her career. It should also be said that, not unexpectedly, the "career profile" has met with considerable opposition because it is thought to be too prescriptive; it has not, therefore, been widely used as a basis for identifying requirements. Finally, none of these models appears to have influenced the ways in which teachers go about identifying their INSET needs.

IV. THE ROLE OF THE SCHOOL

The school is increasingly being seen in many Member countries as a major initiator of and focus for INSET. A justification for school-focused INSET was given by Perry (105) reporting the Stockholm Conference: "The case has been cogently made that to ensure true implementation of change ... we must work with teachers in the place and in the situation where change is to take place. The case is made with equal cogency that the school-building is the context in which all needs at all levels of the system ultimately come together." He also offered a definition. "School-focused training is all the strategies employed by trainers and teachers in partnership to direct training programmes in such a way as to meet the identified needs of the school, and to raise the standards of teaching and learning in the classroom."

A major task has, of course, been to clarify the definition and rationale of school-focused INSET. Howey in his Synthesis Report (25) has demonstrated that the contributions and practical examples in the case studies and conference papers provide a good starting point for this.

In the United Kingdom, a nationally distributed pamphlet (64) suggested several INSET methods of a less conventional kind:

1. A home economics teacher spends a day in another school to find out about a new child-care course.
2. Two deputy heads in a very different primary school exchange jobs for one week to broaden their experience.
3. A large comprehensive school timetable frees staff for one week each year to work on materials preparation with the resource centre co-ordinator.
4. Two colleagues in the same school systematically observe each other teaching over a term and discuss their observations after each session.
5. A group of comprehensive school staff developing a new integrated-studies curriculum

invites a teachers' centre warden to co-ordinate a term-long school-based course involving outside speakers.
6. A college of education offers a week-long course for primary schools for four weeks in succession. Each of four members of staff attend in turn thus having a similar experience. College staff follow-up by visiting the schools.
7. Two LEA advisers offer a school-based course of eight weekly sessions on primary maths. They spend from 3.0 to 3.45 working with teachers in their classrooms and from 4.0 to 5.30 in follow-up workshop/discussion sessions.
8. A university award-bearing course for a group of staff from the same school includes a substantial school-based component.
9. A school runs a conference on "Going Comprehensive" which begins on Friday morning, in school time, and ends on Saturday afternoon. Outside speakers include a chief adviser, a comprehensive head and a university lecturer. As a result, several working parties run throughout the following year."

Wide-ranging examples of school-focused INSET are described in the Australian report (16) and are summarised by Howey (19):

"... short meetings, residential conferences for the entire staff, whole-day activities for the staff held at the school or other venue, visits from consultants, interchange with or visits to other schools, interaction with parents, short conferences (1-3 days), in-depth curriculum study of materials, developmental workshops (2-5 weeks release), whole-term release, activities which examine problems of an organisation or curricular nature that face the staff of a particular school, long-term classroom-based action research with consultancy report, teachers' centre or education centre activities, an extended (developmental) series of meetings, and finally residential in-service education programmes.

Secondary schools in several countries have designated a senior member of staff as the equivalent of a professional tutor. In the United Kingdom, for instance, several local education authorities have encouraged secondary schools to develop their own in-service policies and programmes and to appoint a professional tutor with responsibilities for initial induction and in-service training (vide Baker, 1979), although in most schools these are split between two or more experienced staff. Thus, in one secondary school, a deputy head co-ordinates the professional development programme and concentrates on that aspect aimed at experienced teachers. He is assisted by a less senior colleague who looks after probationary teachers and student teachers. The school's professional development committee is chaired by the deputy head, with the tutor acting as secretary, and the membership is made up of teacher representatives, the LEA's general adviser for the school, and the liaison tutor from a college of education. Examples of similar developments include the introduction of school-based teacher educators in Houston, United States (108) and the proposals for a specific personnel function and in-service plans within Dutch secondary schools (116).

At its best, school-focused INSET is one aspect of a school's staff development policy and thus an integral part of its overall school development policy. The British governmental pamphlet already referred to (64) recommended schools in England and Wales to devise an INSET programme focused on the needs of individual teachers, functional groups (e.g. departmental teams) and the whole school staff. This approach underpins the "site" research project which has been evaluated by Baker (46) and has involved 50 schools.

Fullan (17) describes examples of two school-based INSET activities in Canada:

"... in which the staff play a major role in defining specific school needs, program development requirements and progress in relation to given goals. The district provides time, money, and other forms of support including the use of external consultants. The programs, however, are directed at single, albeit major, problems. We do not get a sense of whether ongoing in-service development at the individual, small group and school level is 'a way of life' regarding all in-service needs of teachers. It is also not clear whether the school as an organisation is a focus for change (i.e. the development of the role of the principal, communication and decision-making skills of staff, etc.). Nonetheless, there is much more emphasis placed on the school qua school as the focal point for development of in-service programs geared toward the particular needs of the staff of individual schools."

In Denmark, a school-based INSET programme was mounted in a primary school by researchers from the Royal Danish School of Educational Studies. Olsen (104) reports that the three-year action-research study aimed "to meet the needs of teachers with regard to content in a realistic setting where you work with colleagues on a team and can draw upon expertise and information from outside geared to your needs and wishes".

Olsen concluded that it took far more time than anticipated to develop fruitful working relationships and for the crucial task of needs definition; that the researchers had to be prepared to adopt an active consultancy role; and, finally, that it was important for the researchers to work collaboratively with teachers in their classrooms.

In Sweden, according to Larsson (95), the move towards school-focused INSET is the natural consequence of a wider trend towards decentralisation of decision-making about school matters. For example, schools involved in the "Local School Development, Planning and Evaluation" project were given complete discretion for planning their five INSET days. One school did so using a working party involving representatives of teachers, non-teaching personnel, students and parents. The preliminary evaluation results indicate that, although the impact of these INSET activities upon the internal work of the school has been limited, they have

> "... contributed to a more intense debate and discussion in educational matters, to a greater openness in the relations between groups and individuals, to better knowledge of the conditions under which their own school works, to a deeper engagement in problems concerning their own situation, and to an increased consciousness of their own responsibility for the solution of these problems".

Other examples of school-focused INSET display features of a more centralised or managerial kind. The Montgomery County staff development programme, for example, is a district level scheme which is based upon specific performance expectations for each teacher, and the Lincoln district uses a variant on management by objectives for its staff appraisal and development scheme (19). In Canada, according to Fullan (17), most school districts "... seem to be primarily concerned about the implementation of provincial curriculum guidelines within which they interpret and set priorities for their own district. There is a tension between accomplishing district wide priorities and individual teacher or school priorities which sometimes do not align with the district emphasis."

The district described by Fullan in one case study has tried to pursue district priorities while treating the school as the main target for change and encouraging each school to work out detailed curriculum procedures and a scale of INSET needs and priorities. A similar approach underlies some recent proposals in the Netherlands (116) and, on a much larger and more generously funded scale, is evident in California (50).

A particular study was made of the actual and potential contribution of teachers' centres to school-focused INSET. As Howey rightly observes in his Synthesis Report (25) there is considerable diversity not only between countries and cultures but within countries in terms of those structures and operations which are referred to as teacher centres. He goes on to argue that -

> "While many teacher centres are school-focussed in nature, others are not. It is difficult to generalise, but the differences between some teachers' centres and other forms of in-service which are specifically school-focussed would include the following:
>
> 1. The primary focus in most teacher centers quite obviously is on teachers; while many school-focussed in-service endeavors tend to attend to the needs of all educational and educationally-related personnel in a school building.
> 2. The focus in many teachers' centers tends to be more on individual teacher needs and interests, while in many school-focussed endeavors there is at least some attention to problems which are best attended to by the entire faculty or close working groups within that faculty.
> 3. Many teacher centers have a district or regional focus; they attend to the needs of a number of schools. Other forms of school-focussed in-service concentrate their energies more directly on individual schools.
> 4. There is an effort in many teacher centers to develop better linkages and co-ordination between and among the plethora of agents and agencies which are to some extent involved in the continuing education of teachers. In other forms of school-focussed in-service a variety of persons external to the school are called upon, but the primary goal is to attend to the needs of the individual school and not serve as a co-ordinating agency.

Thus, it seems reasonable to conclude that, whatever their other undoubted strengths, there is, as yet, no evidence that teachers' centres are any more likely than other providing agencies to offer school-focused INSET. Moreover, given the diversity of teachers' centres referred to above, it may well be more productive to concentrate on identifying effective roles and strategies for school-focused INSET by analysing examples of good practice, wherever these occur, and then disseminating descriptions as widely as possible so that providing agencies of all types can adopt and adapt these methods where appropriate.

For example, external advisers or consultants can manifestly play an important part in school-focused INSET. Ingvarson (16) describes the work of a small team in Victoria, Australia, who visit schools to help teachers to develop and improve mathematics programmes. In New Zealand, each education district has a team of advisers and Forrest (18) describes the priorities of one rural schools adviser as being:

1. Visiting newly-appointed principals.
2. Visiting teachers in response to requests for assistance.
3. Visiting newly-appointed assistants.
4. Visiting teachers to build on ideas initiated on a previous visit or at an in-service course.

In the Netherlands (21), one regional centre works directly with schools which request help on subject teaching. This involves classroom visits and school team meetings. The Detroit Center for Professional Growth and Development has a field consultancy service which helps primary teachers (23). In England, advisory teachers are common and some have particular responsibilties for beginning teachers (100). Detailed national studies of advisory teachers and consultants, particularly in contrast to those advisers with inspectorial functions would thus be of value, as previously suggested by Bolam, Smith and Canter (56).

Following these accounts of practical examples, perhaps the simplest way to summarise and clarify the nature of school-focused INSET is to compare and contrast it with the two commonest alternatives – the long course and the short course. To simplify this comparison the examples are drawn from one country – the United Kingdom – and summarised in Table 1. Long courses there include the in-service B.Ed., and Advanced Diploma in Education and the M.Ed. Characteristically, such courses would:

- last up to three years;
- be located off the school site at a university or college of higher education;
- be staffed by university or college lecturers who would also initiate and design them;
- be attended by individual teachers from different schools;
- be aimed at meeting the professional and, to some extent, the personal educational needs of individual teachers;
- take place away from the teachers' classrooms and schools and thus in an off-the-job or course-embedded context;
- concentrate on conveying knowledge about theory, research and subject disciplines;
- use teaching methods like lectures, tutorials and discussion groups;

Table 1

SCHOOL-FOCUSED INSET COMPARED WITH LONG AND SHORT COURSES

Characteristics	Long Course	Short Course	School-Focused
	e.g. (In-service); B.Ed., Advanced Diploma, and M.Ed.	e.g. 10 weekly sessions at a teachers' centre on subject teaching	e.g. Day conference and follow-up group meetings
Aims	Individual professional/personal development	Individual vocational development	Group/School (i.e. system) development
Location	Centre (i.e. off-site)	Mainly centre	Mainly school (i.e. on site)
Participants	Individual teachers from different schools	Mainly individual teachers from different schools	Individuals and groups mainly from one school
Context	Off-the-job/course embedded	Off-the-job/course embedded	Job related and sometimes on-the-job/job-embedded
Length	Up to 3 years	Up to 12 weeks	Usually short term
Staffing	Centre/external	Mainly centre/external	School and external
Initiator/Designer	Centre	Centre (usually)	School/Group/Teacher
Content	Knowledge of theory, research and subject discipline	General, practical, knowledge and skills	Job specific, problem-solving, practical knowledge and skills
Typical methods	Lectures, tutorials and discussion groups	Workshops, films and simulations	School visits, classroom observations and job rotation
Accreditation/Awards	Yes	Sometimes	Very rarely
Follow-up	Rarely	Sometimes	Usually
Evaluation	Rarely	Sometimes	Sometimes

- normally result in an academic award or accreditation which would often be an aid to a salary increase or promotion;
- rarely involve any follow-up contacts at the end of the course; and
- rarely be evaluated by the providing agency for impact upon teaching performance or school change.

Examples of short courses in the United Kingdom include evening or weekend conferences and courses of, say, 10 weekly two-hour sessions on topics like primary science, school management and in-school evaluation. Characteristically, such courses would:

- last for no more than one term of ten weeks;
- be located mainly, but not exclusively, off the school site at a teachers' centre, college of higher education or university;
- be staffed mainly by staff from this external centre who would normally initiate and design the course;
- be attended mainly by individual teachers from different schools but sometimes by pairs or groups from the same school;
- be aimed at meeting the vocational development needs of individual teachers in the hope that this would improve their work in school;
- take place away from the teachers' classrooms and schools and thus in an off-the-job and course-embedded context;
- concentrate on practical knowledge and skills but at a fairly high level of generality;
- use teaching methods like workshops, simulations and films as well as lectures and discussion groups;
- sometimes lead to an accreditation which may be recognised for promotion (but not salary) purposes;
- sometimes involve follow-up visits by the course staff to the teachers in their schools;
- sometimes be informally evaluated by the providing agency for impact upon teaching performance or school change.

Examples of school-focused INSET activities include staff conferences, and follow-up activities, staff development programmes and consultancy visits. Characteristically, such activities would:

- vary considerably in length but rarely extend beyond one year;
- be mainly school-based but sometimes take place off-site at another school or a teachers' centre, etc.;

- be staffed by teachers from the school and by external advisers and invited contributors or consultants;
- be initiated, and often designed, by the school in the light of school and group policies;
- be attended by individuals, groups or the whole staff from the school and sometimes by outsiders;
- be aimed at the group and whole staff (i.e. system) development needs of the school;
- sometimes but not usually, take place in the classroom or some other on-the-job or job-embedded context;
- concentrate on practical knowledge and skills of a job-specific and problem-solving kind;
- use experience-based "teaching" methods like job rotation, classroom observation by peers, visits to other schools and organisation development, as well as lectures, discussions, films, etc.;
- only rarely lead to any kind of award, accreditation, salary increase or promotion;
- normally involve follow-up work as an integral part of the activity; and
- sometimes be informally evaluated by school staff for impact upon teaching performance and school change.

The comparative, operational characterisation of school-focused INSET should be read alongside the earlier one quoted above from Perry (105) and the definition in Howey's Synthesis Report (25):

"In summary, school-focused in-service can be defined as those continuing education activities which focus upon the interest, needs and problems directly related to one's role and responsibilities in a specific school site. These forms of in-service focus not only on individual teacher concerns and needs, but on matters which demand the co-ordinated efforts of several, if not all, persons in a specific school setting. When appropriate, both members of the larger school community and the student population should have input into decisions about necessary changes in the school and their implications for INSET. These forms of in-service commonly call for changes in the organisational structure and programmatic nature of a school. They have implications for basic role as well as specific behavioural changes. These forms of in-service should take place in the form of an articulated framework which considers dimensions of the organisational/sociological nature of the school and the curriculum and instructional patterns within which teachers work. The basic psychological growth as well as the professional development of the teacher should also be considered."

From the evidence of these definitions and the national case studies it seems reasonable to conclude that "school-focused" is a term which describes a loose orientation to INSET, rather than a conceptually rigorous strategy for it. Nevertheless, it has helped to establish the existence of the international agreement about the urgent need for INSET to be more relevant to teachers' jobs and to the pressing needs of schools as organisations. Furthermore, it has helped to clarify the widely-held view that the traditional INSET strategy, whereby individual teachers attend courses provided by outside agencies, is valuable but too limited and that it should be deliberately extended to encourage teachers and school staffs to plan their own INSET programmes in the light of their self-identified needs.

Beyond this basic but generally agreed standpoint different emphases and several unresolved issues are apparent. The conclusions reached in Howey's Synthesis Report that school-focused INSET occurs infrequently and is unlikely to expand rapidly are important and prompt the question: "Why should this be, given that the method is apparently so popular with teachers?" Conceptual, economic, financial, logistical, professional and organisational reasons are likely to be relevant to varying degrees in particular countries. Howey argues convincingly that informed and funded support is essential, particularly at local school levels. Moreover, if it is considered important that higher education institutions should modify their approach to encompass school-focused INSET, then their internal organisation and incentive structures will have to be changed so that college lecturers see it as worthwhile to engage in school-focused work as well as in more traditional courses.

Not unexpectedly, the apparently straightforward question, "How cost-effective is school-focused INSET?" is soon revealed as a complex and multidimensional one. At least four main variables have to be specified in assessing the cost-effectiveness of any INSET activity: aims, length, staffing and teacher release and replacement requirements. As we shall see, the limited evidence at present available (which generally does not control for these four variables) indicates that specified forms of INSET which would come within Howey's definition, are more cost-effective for certain purposes.

A third set of issues relates to the notion of on-the-job or job-embedded INSET. First, it should be said that a generally acceptable distinction can be drawn between on-the-job and on-site INSET. An activity may take place on the school premises (i.e. on-site) without being on-the-job. Thus, a management course for heads of department held in the staff room after school would be on-site (or school-based) but not in an on-the-job context. On the other hand, an advisory teacher observing and advising a new teacher as she taught her class would be on-the-job (or job-embedded) training. Next, although it is the case that much of what happens throughout the normal day, for instance staff meetings and team teaching, could be said to lead to professional development, it is surely more helpful to adopt a definition of INSET, such as Henderson's (81), based upon intentionality: "... activities which are designed, exclusively or primarily, to improve and extend the professional capabilities of teachers". Thus a staff meeting would only count as job-embedded or on-the-job INSET if that was its prime purpose.

However, although these conceptual difficulties can be relatively easily overcome, the practical difficulties of extending job-embedded INSET are often more intractable. For example, the teacher tutors in the United Kingdom induction schemes were reluctant to enter the classrooms of their probationers in case this diminished the latter's professional status in the eyes of the pupils (55). In any case, the tutors frequently could not find the time to engage in classroom-based INSET and this, too, is a major obstacle to job-embedded work as the Synthesis Report indicates (25).

A fourth issue arises from the fact that, by its very nature, school-focused INSET is likely to give priority to the needs of the school as a system over those of the individual teacher. Moreover, this is likely to be particularly true at a time of economic crisis: local authorities and school principals are likely to allocate scarce resources, especially that of release time, to INSET activities which can be justified to their pay-masters as having direct relevance to school needs. In consequence, activities related primarily to the career needs of individual teachers are likely to suffer.

V. TRAINING THE TRAINERS

As Mulford points out in his Synthesis Report (32), it is widely acknowledged that those who provide INSET could benefit from some form of training. For example, a particular study was made of the training needs of teacher tutors with responsibilities for providing school-based INSET for beginning teachers during pilot schemes in England and Wales. Whereas, at the outset of the project, there were uncertainties about both the need for and content of tutor training, by the end the case for training teacher tutors was made most forcibly: 71 per cent of all respondents agreed that tutors needed some form of training. Tutors themselves were most convinced of this, especially those from secondary schools (94 per cent). However, only 53 per cent of tutors considered the training they had received had been adequate: 87 per cent said that the LEA should also produce written guidelines for tutors and 69 per cent thought that on-going and not simply preparatory training was necessary (55).

Perhaps the first task within any country is to reach some agreement about who the INSET trainers are. Three distinctions are worth making at the outset: between those who are based inside and those who are based outside schools; between those for whom INSET is their primary or exclusive job and those for whom it is a secondary or incidental part of their job; and between those who are seen by teachers as employer representatives (e.g. inspectors) and those who are not.

Within schools, it is rare for someone to have INSET as their principal job but in large secondary schools there is an increasing tendency for a senior staff member (e.g. a deputy principal) to have staff development as a major job component. This is true in the United Kingdom (45) and has been strongly recommended in the Netherlands (46). In Texas, the role of school-based teacher educators has been the subject of research and according to Howey (85) the following roles have been identified: "resource specialists, design and development specialists, supervisors of prospective teachers, team leaders, teacher training design and development and other specialised supervisory positions."

This list serves to illustrate the point that within schools a number of people have varying degrees of responsibility for staff development and INSET. Principals and department heads fall into this category but so, too, do newer types of role like the Japanese school-based research co-ordinator (5) and the English primary teachers who act as internal advisory or resource personnel to their colleagues for a specialist subject area like science.

Mulford (32) reaches the following conclusion:

"With outside expertise coming under increasing criticism and the swing to school focused/based INSET becoming more pronounced, the role of <u>insiders to the school</u> (headmaster and teachers) in the training of INSET trainers has become important. However, the role of the headmaster in this training poses a dilemma - on the one hand there is mounting research evidence indicating the key role played by the headmaster in effective change, on the other hand, there is evidence that headmasters (and district consultants and supervisors) are not rated highly by teachers as INSET instructors. The resolution of this dilemma appears to lie in the suggestion that although the headmaster is vital for facilitating INSET, the actual training should be carried out by teachers.
Unfortunately, the evidence and suggestions that teachers be given the pre-eminent voice in INSET should not be construed that they also desire to be, or are currently competent as, INSET trainers. Only a small proportion of teachers would like to teach in-service courses and when they do they tend both to instruct rather than stimulate or encourage and have problems of legitimacy and expertise in the eyes of their peers - particularly those who are closest. Research implies that people in schools need to learn and re-learn ways of working together, and of sharing power and decision-making."

Encouragingly, new ways that can work effectively with peers have been reported. Batten (47) says that an element that emerges strongly from consideration of the variety of in-service activities encompassed by this report is the importance of peer-group influence. The word of the informed teacher, or parent, or administrator is likely to be heeded and acted upon by the peer group more readily than information received from any other source. He adds that the opportunity to observe other teachers in action, through school visits or teacher exchange, has been found by teachers to be a useful in-service activity and could be included by more development committees in their policy-making and planning. Other examples include the use of peer group panels (97):

"- They act as a sounding board for one another's self-analysis of needs, and for ideas and plans for improvement.
- They assist each other in analysing teaching and curriculum, often by systematic observing in each other's classrooms - using low inference measures;
- They give one another low inference feedback on behaviour observed or work analysed, and
- They verify 'for the record', if a record of competence development is needed, the member's attaining of an objective in his/her improvement plan."

The term "low inference" is used to describe observation judgements and feedback based upon a pre-agreed set of relatively objective categories. "High inference" judgements are seen as counter-productive.

Outside schools, an equally varied number of personnel act as INSET trainers. Often they are employed by the local or national authority. For example, in a study of fourteen English local authorities by Bolam, Smith and Canter (56), particular attention was given to the training needs of local authority advisers and inspectors, most of whom spend a great deal of their time providing INSET. Less than 15 per cent of those questioned had received any specific training yet almost 70 per cent recommended that advisers should receive specific training. Partly to overcome the difficulties caused by the inspectorial aspects of such roles, many national, state and local systems have introduced some form of advisory teacher whose main job is INSET, especially for primary schools. For example, in the United States, Rauh (107) describes the work of instructional associates and Howey (85) summarises work on the advisory teachers' role; Groenhagen (21) outlines the ways in which members of the guidance service provided by the Dutch local and regional education centres visit and help teachers in schools; McMahon (100) describes the induction role of advisory teachers in England; Ingvarson (16) describes the work of a (maths advisory) team in Australia; and Forrest (18) provides a very useful cast-study of an adviser to rural primary schools in New Zealand.

Three general observations are worth making about the advisory teacher role: first, it appears to be an effective way of providing a formal framework within which experienced specialist teachers can help colleagues; second, it seems to work best in primary schools; third, teachers appear to respond well to the role, from which one may conclude that the role is a potent one which is worthy of more widespread adoption.

Another major group of INSET trainers are in the institutions of higher education - colleges, polytechnics and universities. Mulford (32) concludes that the place of outsiders to the system, particularly those from higher education, seems limited in the eyes of teachers. They complain, he says, that personnel from higher education institutions are poorly prepared to help, lack credibility, lack mutual understanding and are too remote and theoretical particularly when school-based activities are preferred.

There is undoubtedly considerable force and validity in this conclusion but it does require some qualification. First, there is reason to believe that teachers' opinions of college staff are frequently based on stereotypes and, moreover, that, when teachers and college staff actually work together on INSET activities, these stereotypes can be eroded and that much more favourable opinions result (46 and 100). Second, there is ample evidence that, particularly as a result of the drop in initial teacher training numbers, college staffs are reviewing their roles and adopting a much more outward-looking and school-oriented stance (46, 47, 65). Third, in several countries universities and colleges play little part in INSET and it is at least arguable that this is an under-utilisation of valuable professional resources.

A second important consideration for Member countries is to ask what INSET trainers actually do, and might reasonably be expected to do. Relatively few systematic or comprehensive surveys have been reported though there are several exceptions. For example, in the United States, Katz (92) studied the role and functions of advisers; in the United Kingdom, Bolam, Smith and Canter (56) reported on a study of local advisers and inspectors with particular reference to INSET and innovation while the functions and training needs of professional tutors have also been studied by Bolam, Baker and McMahon (55); in the Netherlands the roles of internal support officials or change agents have been surveyed (116). The research on school-based teacher educators (SBTE) in the United States is one of the most interesting of these studies because the extremely thorough review and analysis led to a list of competencies with direct implications for training needs (84):

> "The resulting set of 20 competency specifications assumed that an SBTE would be able to perform, as a teacher, the specified competencies as well as facilitate their performance by others. SBTEs:
> 1. assist teachers to develop interpersonal skills and effective communication with students, colleagues and school constituencies;
> 2. assist teachers to gather and utilize relevant data about school, classroom, and community environments;

3. assist teachers to understand and work effectively with different socio-economic/ethnic/cultural groups;
4. assist teachers to translate knowledge of current educational research and development into instructional practices;
5. assist teachers to develop a personal teaching style consistent with their own philosophy;
6. assist teachers to develop their understanding of basic concepts and theories of the subjects they teach;
7. assist teachers to understand and use techniques and instruments designed to diagnose students' academic and social development needs;
8. assist teachers to design, develop, and maintain environments that facilitate learning;
9. assist teachers to develop instructional goals and objectives;
10. assist teachers to develop and/or adapt instructional programs and materials;
11. assist teachers to select and utilize various strategies and models of teaching, for example, concept development, inductive procedures, non-directive teaching;
12. assist teachers to design and implement personalised learning plans;
13. assist teachers to develop effective leadership skills;
14. assist teachers to understand and use effective techniques of classroom management;
15. assist teachers to evaluate instructional effectiveness by collecting, analyzing and interpreting data on teacher and student behavior;
16. assist teachers to develop, implement, and assess continuing individual professional growth plans;
17. plan and conduct individual conferences with teachers;
18. recognise the existence of personal problems that affect a teacher's instructional effectiveness and initiate appropriate referral process;
19. demonstrate effective planning, organisation, and management skills;
20. facilitate research studies on teaching and learning.

A third major consideration for Member countries is to review the range of available INSET methods and to assess their relevance and effectiveness. Not unexpectedly the reports and case studies include accounts of an extremely varied range of techniques including clinical supervision, organisation development, micro-teaching, classroom analysis, simulations, competency-based methods and distance-teaching. Thus, quite apart from the substantive subject-matter (e.g. mathematics teaching) which the trainer may be trying to communicate, there are numerous methods and techniques with which, ideally, they would be familiar. An early plea was made for an analytic and critical typology of INSET methods (11) but the difficulties of producing one are considerable. A preliminary attempt distinguishes between multi-media productions, restricted media presentations, media emphasising written presentation, single small-scale aids and small-scale training systems and media (31).

However, even a typology at this level of generality is difficult to apply to the numerous approaches described in the case studies. Three of the eighteen cases summarised by Mulford (32) illustrate this point: first, the school-based project in Denmark in which university lecturers worked in a consultancy style with a group of teachers from a school who themselves decided the programme of study (104); second, the IT/INSET project in the United Kingdom in which teams consisting of two experienced teachers, one college lecturer and five initial training student teachers work together in a school to promote self-evaluation and professional development for all three groups (Henderson et al, 79); and third, the Swedish School Leader Education Project in which the training was based on interaction between leaders and on activities which included some periods of self-observation (66).

Two further indications of the difficulties of devising a satisfactory typology are worthy of attention. First is the tendency for any discussion of INSET methods and materials to be dominated by considerations related to distance-learning and hardware-based techniques like micro-teaching. Important as these are, their utility is limited. The vast majority of INSET activities are far more likely to be characterised by face-to-face interactions between trainer and teacher and hence it is help with the methodology or pedagogy of these interactions which will be of most value to the INSET trainer. Second, we may note the continuing debate about the concept of consultancy. For instance in considering the implications of consultancy for INSET several experienced practitioners and researchers in the United Kingdom have expressed doubts about the relevance and helpfulness of typologies based on a "pure" non-directive model of consultancy (78). Eraut (68) writes as follows:

> "I am adopting a very broad definition of consultant and abandoning the implicit assumption in my earlier writings that a consultant is necessarily non-directive. This avoids problems of exclusion by definition and leaves me free to examine a wide range of possible consultancy roles.

My definition, therefore, is that a consultant is any external agent from within the educational system who involves himself in discussing the educational problems of a class, department or school with a view to improving the quality of teaching and learning. I mean to exclude lay people from this definition unless they are effectively co-professional - some journalists and authors might belong in this category."

In this definition the potential "consultancy" contributions of a whole range of professionals (e.g. inspectors) can be re-examined - an important resource factor - but the pure concept of consultancy has to be modified with direct implications for, amongst other methods, clinical supervision and organisation development.

A fourth major consideration is for Member countries to ask what kind of training should be established for INSET trainers. In his review of eighteen case studies, Mulford (32) points out that training occurs in a wide variety of settings: for example, in Portugal a centre has been established to define the training needs and has run experimental seminars on group dynamics and pedagogical evaluation, while in France integrated centres for training adult trainers have been set up. He concludes that most of the material here tended to emphasise the general factors that training should take into consideration rather than specific methodologies. These general factors were synthesised into eight points: the need to be aware of schools as organisations, the nature of teachers and teaching, the school's context, the trainer input dilemma and andragogy (adult learning theory) and emphasis on participatory approaches, experiential learning and educational administrator training.

Given the wide variety of settings, roles, functions and methods which have been outlined in this section, the most important single consideration is that training courses for INSET trainers (just as for teachers) should be as context-specific as possible. It follows that, if materials and training packages are to be produced either nationally or internationally, it is essential that they should be capable of adaptation to local and individual circumstances and that ways of facilitating such adaptation should be built in from the outset.

VI. COSTS, FINANCES AND RESOURCES

One of the most important yet intractably problematic aspects of INSET is that of obtaining reliable information about costs. As Kaplan (38) says in his Synthesis Report: "The study of costs of INSET activities is perhaps the area in which results are farthest from expectations. One hopes for a multitude of hard facts and figures and for at least a few indisputable generalisations. Instead, one finds that relatively few things can be said objectively on this subject, for the reasons mentioned in the introduction: lack and dispersion of data and non-comparability of programs. Added to this is the fact that INSET is often an ongoing activity of teachers and administrators carried on concurrently with other activities, so that its costs are often not clearly separated out."

This is true of both centralised and decentralised systems. According to Henricson (37) even in a centralised system like the Swedish one, it is, for many reasons, not possible to reach an exact overall calculation of the cost of INSET. In some cases where the total costs can be determined it is not possible to allocate the expenditure to specific types of costs.

In England and Wales, a 1978 government survey (63) encountered similar problems: "... local authorities had not been able to keep their records in a form which enabled them to answer all the questions precisely and replies to some of the questions were estimates. Further, some questions raised difficulties of definition and measurement of costs and could not be answered on a uniform basis as between authority and authority. These difficulties were apparent particularly in regard to the involvement in induction and in-service training of members of local authority advisory services where in some instances their costs had to be imputed."

The fact that this was the first such survey in England and Wales exemplifies a distinct trend in Member countries, many of which are seeking to clarify the major cost components of INSET. However, the general impression gained from the case studies is that only limited progress has been made, as a comparison with the categories used for costing higher education reveals. Thus, a study at the University of Sussex (106) distinguishes between capital and recurrent costs and between social and internal opportunity costs but such distinctions do not figure explicitly in the British document just quoted, nor in most of the case studies.

An Australian study is a notable exception, but although Cameron (34) gives the capital costs for certain aspects of INSET (e.g. for education centres), he deals mainly with recurrent costs. Moreover, all the studies have difficulty in differentiating between the proportions of recurrent costs which should be allocated to INSET and to, say, curriculum development or school inspection. A solution adopted in the British document was to impute the INSET proportion of advisers' salaries but the precise criteria used and their validity are unclear.

The reasons for these costing problems arise mainly from the lack of a clear INSET structure, from the sheer range of institutions and agencies which provide INSET, from the diversity of their programmes and activities, each with their own often unclear goals and purposes, and from the different patterns of teacher participation. In most Member countries, the INSET system, unlike the initial training system, is in a state of flux and development and the responsibilities for financing it are unclear. Hence firm definitions and distinctions are simply not possible at this stage.

It should, however, be possible to make some fundamental conceptual distinctions that have practical value. One such distinction is that between costs questions (e.g. How much does course X cost?) and finance questions (e.g. Who pays these costs?). A second distinction is that between accounting and planning costs. As Westoby says in his Management in Education Course at the Open University (117):

> "Putting it very broadly therefore 'accounting' costs are the outcome of retrospective or historical allocations of resources which have already been used (or at least irreversibly allocated) to particular goals and activities, whereas 'planning' costing is concerned principally with those resources which are the real subject of choice since they have not yet been (finally) committed (and could therefore in principle be avoided or transferred to some other purpose). Frequently of course some costs derived for 'accounting' purposes are used as estimates of costs for 'planning' purposes."

A third distinction is that between the costs of provision or supply (e.g. How much does it cost to provide course X ?) and of take-up or demand (e.g. How much does it cost to attend and participate in course X ?).

These distinctions generate four basic questions:

- What did the provision and take-up of "Y" cost?
- Who paid for the provision and take-up of "Y"?
- What should the provision and take-up of "Y" cost?
- Who should pay for the provision and take-up of "Y"?

In these examples, "Y" could be an INSET activity, course, programme or agency/institution. In principle, it ought to be possible to identify the major cost components to answer the accounting costs questions for INSET within and between Member countries, although the relevant data will not always be available. The answers to the financing and planning questions will probably be much more culture-bound but here, too, the broad categories should be identifiable.

Cameron (34) for Australia, distinguishes between four major types of recurrent costs for short courses and workshops: assembly costs, including those of accommodation and travel; replacement costs, to cover the salaries of substitutes for participating teachers; administration costs, which cover the salaries of general administrative and clerical staff and of general office supplies and postage; and organisation costs, which cover lecturers' fees, materials and equipment for specific courses. He estimates the average distribution of these costs as:

Assembly	20 - 25 per cent
Replacement	60 - 65 per cent
Administration	10 - 12 per cent
Organisation	8 - 12 per cent

In this example the costs of provision and take-up amount to 18-24 per cent and 80-90 per cent respectively.

Bradley (33) outlines the costs of a five-day residential course in the United Kingdom and, collapsing his categories into ones similar to Cameron's, the following approximate percentages emerge:

Assembly	20
Replacement	73
Administration	?
Organisation	7

As far as one can tell, administrative costs do not appear explicitly in the British list. It is also unclear whether Cameron's "Assembly" category includes the travel costs of the lecturers (i.e. the providers). These were included in "Organisation" category for the United Kingdom in order to preserve the distinction between provision and take-up; on this basis, one can say that the provision costs were 7 per cent while take-up costs were 93 per cent.

The detailed accuracy of these examples is less important at this stage than the broader issues which they raise. For, if meaningful comparisons of accounting costs for INSET are to be made within and between countries, at least three conditions must be met. First, the categories being costed must be defined and agreed. Second, the relative merits of different types of unit costs should be explored and appropriate ones agreed: some of the studies use costs per teacher, some use costs per full-time teacher, the American report (35) suggests costs per training hour, and another possibility is costs per teacher hour. Third, the costs must be presented in percentages as well as currency figures. Only when these and similar conditions are met will it be possible to make informed judgements about the relative costs of each component, and of the costs of different types of INSET. At present, and certainly in the Australian and British examples quoted above, teachers' replacement salaries appear to be the costliest item by far; but as long as capital costs are excluded from the calculations the full significance of this high recurrent cost must remain obscure. Similarly, only when these items have been clarified will it be possible to assess the feasibility and desirability of introducing the concept of opportunity costs into the calculations.

Kaplan in his Synthesis Report (38) offers the following generalisations about patterns of financing INSET in individual countries:

> "Three of the five countries studied handle education in general and INSET in particular in a basically decentralised fashion. In these countries, central government financing is aimed more at new and innovative programs; in some cases, this financing is growing in importance. These funds have often been helpful in starting or maintaining teacher centers. Central governments also support INSET indirectly through more general grants to local educational or government authorities and through financial support to colleges and universities. Yet it is local authorities which are the main financers of INSET. They pay most replacement costs and provide most administrative and some specialist personnel for local courses. Colleges and universities are the third biggest source of funds in these countries. Teachers as individuals also contribute large amounts of time to INSET, although this is hard to total up. Other financers of INSET include teachers' unions and subject associations, other government units, private businesses and foundations."

The financial and planning questions – Who pays and who ought to pay? – raise wider issues which have to be considered from various viewpoints. For, as Pickford (106) demonstrates, the decisions that precede and follow costing exercises are crucially influenced by the viewpoint adopted. It is, therefore, of considerable practical importance to review INSET costs from various perspectives, although this is by no means easy as is evident from the reports, several of which predominantly reflect a national perspective.

In considering teacher time as a major cost item, for example, it is obviously vital to look at it from the teachers', as well as from the employers', standpoint. Teacher time is a major INSET resource and teachers' perspectives on this and other costs should help our understanding of their motivation towards INSET and of whether or not particular incentives are likely to be effective. At one extreme, the fact that a teacher has to pay her own fees and travel expenses to attend a course in her own time could act as a powerful disincentive; at the other extreme, the fact that a teacher's employer would pay all course fees and travel expenses for a course held in school time could act as a powerful incentive. In several countries it is undoubtedly the case that more teachers attend INSET in their own time than in their employer's time. For example, in the United Kingdom more than half the teachers undertaking training had been doing so as part of their overall professional responsibility and without absence from normal classroom activities (63). In Denmark it was difficult to assess the total extent of this activity, but it was "surprisingly large" (36).

Yet, since teacher time appears to be the biggest single recurrent cost of INSET, it is surely important to establish more precisely how much time teachers contribute themselves. This is necessary nationally and also at school level. According to Baker (45) in the United Kingdom:

> "The most significant cost for schools is the teacher time required for involvement in INSET. Time away from normal teaching duties is regarded as potentially disruptive to the school system itself and as a potential loss for the classes normally taken by the teacher. Substitution has to be arranged, possibly on days when several staff are absent for other reasons, and if internal cover is required it may be seen as an 'irritant' by colleagues who have to lose their non-teaching periods. Such factors, coupled with doubts among a proportion of the teaching force about the value of INSET, soon act as checks upon increasing the level of INSET activities as has been evident in one or two project schools. Yet school records to show the extent and distribution of absence among staff, the reasons for it and the classes affected by it,

are not commonly kept in detail or, if kept, are often not in a form allowing easy retrieval of the data to answer these questions.

Baker analysed the daily substitution lists in an English secondary school over a one-year period and found that only 1 per cent of timetabled periods were lost for INSET reasons compared with 2.7 per cent for staff illness. Furthermore, 79 per cent of the INSET undertaken did not require replacement teachers. These figures highlight several issues, not least the need for schools to work out methods of costing their INSET activities.

Whether or not teachers are released for INSET also has important implications for the use of providing agency resources. Traditionally, the undergraduate and graduate education courses provided by colleges and universities depend upon an identifiable group of students attending for a required period, mainly full-time, during the day. Part-time courses often pose major financing problems. Again, taking the United Kingdom as an example:

> "Part of the problem arises because in allocating its funds the University Grants Committee does not at present take full account of work that universities do with part-time students. Increasing the number of students on part-time courses does not necessarily mean that additional grant is received. Indeed, given that total numbers of home-based students are fixed, any substitution of full-timers by part-timers threatens a loss of income.
> Even more seriously, the fees that universities charge for 'public service' part-time courses are such that the total 'unit of resource' (grant plus fees) for part-time students is only a fraction of that for full-timers. A teacher doing a full-time post-graduate MA course at a university next year will pay a fee of £1,105. Each university fixes its own part-time fees, but in some places a part-timer could take the same course over two years for as little as £150 a year. In some public sector colleges which have advanced qualifications validated by universities the tuition fee for the same course is only £5 each year."(114)

The possibilities for colleges to operate more flexibly, say in a school-focused mode, are also constrained by financial and costing procedures; as an American writer argues (65):

> "The work measurement unit used for funding college programs is typically the student credit hour or full-time equivalent student (FTE). The

FTE usually is based upon classroom contact hours for on-campus instruction. This practice assumes that formal instruction in a college classroom in a course format is <u>the</u> way for students to learn and for professors to teach. Courses offered off-campus through offices of field service or extension commonly are taught as an overload, providing the faculty member with extra income. Although some states have adopted 'continuing education units' (CEUs) as a basis for calculating off-campus load or productivity, these, too, conceptualize the professor's work as the teaching of formal college-type courses."

At local authority or employer level it is especially necessary to distinguish between the various types of INSET for which teachers are actually released. Three types were distinguished earlier: long courses leading to an academic award, short courses of a practical nature and school-focused activities. It was also argued that, in a period of economic recession, employing authorities would cut back on teacher release for longer courses first but that, within that category, they would give preference to practically oriented courses which they thought would bring direct and immediate gains to schools.

At national and local levels the issue of teacher release is bound to be a crucial one. Teachers' associations regard it as the litmus test for judging how serious governments actually are about their commitment to INSET. The Swedish teachers' unions, for example, claim that all INSET activities should take place in school time (37). In the United Kingdom, the "James Report" recommended a national figure of 3 per cent release for longer courses, excluding release for shorter courses, but teacher associations now regard this principle as having been seriously eroded by the apparent re-interpretation of the 3 per cent figure to include release for shorter courses.

At a time of severe financial cutbacks it is inevitable that release for INSET should be curtailed but, alongside this economic fact of life, the central importance of release as a professional issue remains potent. As the quotation from the Swedish report implies, fundamental questions about the nature of a teacher's conditions of service are raised by the release issue. Associated with it is the question of who should pay, in terms of course fees as well as time, for the two principal types of INSET: that which is intended mainly for individual professional development and that which is intended mainly for school or system development.

In the United Kingdom Taylor (114) argues that the relevant costs need to be apportioned on a rational basis, which balances individual and social benefits, motivates institutions to provide courses of the kind needed to bring about improvements in teaching, and encourages individuals to take advantage of this provision.

However, the difficulties of achieving such an apportionment are likely to be considerable, as the American report (35) demonstrates: "In one locality a university course may be considered a legitimate INSET expense, paid for by a school district, while in another there may be legislation barring use of INSET funds for college courses."

It is within this context of some uncertainty about INSET costs, and sometimes heated discussions about who should pay, that various possibilities for making more effective use of INSET resources are being explored. Three examples illustrate this point. First, at school level a number of developments are notable. Several countries now finance a specified number of INSET days for whole staffs. In Sweden five such days have been set aside as study days since 1962. In Denmark every school and its staff has four whole days per year, where they can plan their own arrangement of INSET and there is money to pay external experts for their contributions.

In Australia, the Schools Commission's INSET Programme provides funds, disbursed through Regional INSET Committees, which are available to school staffs wishing to run their own INSET programmes (16). In the Netherlands, the Dutch Catholic Schools Council has proposed a differentiated system of financing for external support to schools which would include an element for INSET over which the school would have control (116). Devices like these for stimulating INSET at school level ought to be the subject of separate study.

Second, although a number of methods have been tried to stimulate and facilitate the effective use of providing agency resources, these have not been without problems. In the United Kingdom, two-ninths of staff time in colleges of education was designated for INSET purposes partly with the aim of involving them in school-focused work but, for the reasons elaborated in an American context by Drummond (65), most colleges have used their staffing allocation for conventional courses. The ways in which the roles of potential providing agencies are defined, both by their members and by outsiders, can be important. For example, in the Netherlands, the inspectorate, the universities and the initial training institutions have not played a central role in INSET but their potential contribution is currently under review (93).

Third, a variety of approaches is being adopted to improve arrangements for consultation, collaboration and participation in INSET planning, implementation and evaluation. School-focused INSET is central to many of these approaches, especially where the emphasis is upon teacher-defined needs and programmes. Similarly, the teachers' centre movement, especially in the United States, reflects a concern to give teachers greater control over the programmes. The project's Interim Report (11) identified five main governance task areas:

 a) Release and financing of teachers to undertake INSET.
 b) Content and methods of INSET programmes and activities.
 c) Validation of INSET awards.
 d) Accreditation and certification related to INSET awards.
 e) Co-ordination of INSET provision.

Although the information available about recent developments is sparse, the impression from the reports is that progress has been made on b) to e) but that decision about release and finance largely remain the prerogative of employing authorities. One development is apparent, however, especially in the United States and Australia where there is evidence of increasing involvement of parent and community groups both in decisions about INSET and in the activities themselves (89),(34).

 Finally, in this context, the Synthesis Report (38) highlights an important paradox. Is it possible (writes Kaplan) for the central government to initiate, to fund, to encourage INSET, without creating great resentment by appearing to control and to reduce local powers at a time when many are asking for more local powers? Should we view any change as necessarily bringing resistance? If INSET becomes involved in an I win-you lose political power struggle between central and local government, this resistance is inevitable, and collaboration very difficult. Yet there are perhaps other ways of approaching the question. This international study has revealed the paradoxical necessity for central government funding and encouragement of INSET with as little central government control as possible. Those engaged in dialogue between central and local governments on INSET planning might want to take this point of view into account. A further step in the dialogue (he concludes) might be to ask: Is it possible to create national INSET structures which explicitly recognise this paradox?

VII. EVALUATION: TECHNIQUES AND POLICIES

With the growth in commitment to INSET has come a series of questions about evaluation which usually stem from one or both of two concerns. First, there is a concern that INSET should offer value for money, which we may call the concern for programme accountability. Second, there is a concern to improve the quality of INSET, which we may call the concern for programme improvement. Both concerns have direct implications for the purposes, nature and methodology of evaluation.

Quite understandably, the principal and fundamental concern of those who have to provide the resources for INSET is whether it brings value for money. In the United Kingdom, for instance, local authority advisers need to be able to convince local politicians that it is worth spending money on INSET rather than on reducing the size of classes or on some other social service like housing. Ideally, they would like "hard" information about the effects of a particular INSET programme on teacher performance and, even better, on pupil or student performance. In practice it has not proved easy to provide this type of product or outcomes information. Most evaluations have asked teachers to make a follow-up judgement, either immediately at the end of a course or perhaps a month afterwards, about the impact of the course. When these self-reports have been checked independently, however, their reliability is shown to be questionable. For example, Henderson (80) found little evidence to support the self-reported changes in teachers' behaviour following a distance-teaching course on reading improvement.

It is technically possible to obtain convincing "product" data about effectiveness if some form of competency measurement approach is adopted. Writing from an American perspective, Borich (26) outlines three evaluation models based upon a definition of competency which is tied to a validated and confirmed "relationship between a teaching behaviour and a pupil outcome". Experience in Europe indicates that it is rarely feasible to use such sophisticated instruments and evaluation designs because they are expensive, because the course being evaluated is usually not amenable to a behavioural approach and because programme improvement data is both easier to obtain by other methods and is more highly valued.

The issues are posed very clearly in Eklund's Swedish study (28). For example, it refers to a shift towards what could be called a <u>participatory INSET evaluation</u> model. This change is qualitative in nature and can be seen as a reflection of a general trend discernible in a great many fields. Characteristic features of the model are, among other things:

- the broadening of the field of evaluation so that product evaluation is just one of the components;
- INSET and INSET evaluation as an integrated part of the total school development programme;
- evaluation programmes as decentralised, group-focused and field-centred activities;
- INSET evaluation as an information service to the participants about the characteristics of the school's whole development programme and thus a basis for participatory planning and decision-making.

Eklund goes on to argue, with respect to data collection methods, that

"If you know – and have been able to control – relevant background and situation variables (frames, processes, etc.) the products of a training period provide an excellent basis for evaluation – you need no more. You have a kind of one-dimensional evaluation situation (summative and product-centred). On the other hand, if you are uncertain which variables are the relevant ones (which variables you have been able to hold constant), the mere study of results becomes somewhat pointless. In this case you also need information that makes it possible to estimate the congruence between aims and the didactical model and between the didactical model and the actual behaviour. You get a <u>multi-dimensional evaluation</u> situation (formative and process-centred)."

Essentially then, the argument turns upon the importance attached, on the one hand, to obtaining formative process evaluation information about the ways in which a programme was implemented to inform decisions about programme improvement and, on the other, to obtaining summative, product information about the effectiveness and outcomes of a programme to inform decisions about whether or not to continue with it.

Process data and "soft" product data (e.g. follow-up evaluation) are technically easy to obtain, are relatively cheap and satisfy some "professionals" but few "politicians"; "hard" product data are technically difficult to obtain, are more expensive and are more likely to satisfy the "politicians" but threaten the "professionals". Borich (26) is therefore right to stress that "the 'best' evaluation methodology is dictated by context and dependent upon resources at hand, time and commitment of those conducting the study, requirements and policies shaping the evaluation, and, of course, the objectives of the training institution." It is, incidentally, worth noting that neither these issues nor the technical problems of evaluating INSET are particularly unusual: they have already been confronted in the evaluation of curriculum development and social action programmes - vide Stake (111) and Jenkins (87) - and have given rise to similar debates and rival solutions. Nevertheless, as Fox's Synthesis Report says, it is doubtful whether this experience is being adequately drawn upon (30).

Fox goes on to say that there are three main reasons given for the support of INSET: stimulating professional development, improving school practice and implementing social policy - and three main settings in which INSET occurs - in single schools, multiple schools and ad hoc groups. Moreover, he says that a meaningful discussion of evaluation must take account of these contextual features:

> "... there are two significant parts to the context of our in-service education and training programs: 1. that created by the three reasons we use to support in-service education and training and 2. the settings in which these programs are performed. To articulate or analyze our experience, to judge our effectiveness, to compare, contrast or accumulate what we have learned from our experience in in-service education and training will take a precise identification of what our intentions are and what the setting is. If we discuss only the setting, for example, important features of our own experience are left uncritically analyzed."

Of the many problems which evaluators encounter, Fox highlights three: the bureaucratic context of evaluation, the choice of evaluation methodology and the ambiguity of "participation". One important issue arising from the bureaucratic context is the "political" nature of INSET. Of this he says that the political process in a bureaucracy is focused on how to deal with professionals who represent conflicting but powerful interests. In evaluating in-service education and training, a variety of conflicting professional interests may be affected and many bureaucratic levels may be involved. Thus, from a bureaucratic viewpoint, the evaluation of in-service education and training is a highly political activity.

Fox stresses that a range of options is open to the evaluator:

> "... there are many ways in which an in-service education and training program can be investigated. There are a variety of case study traditions. There are quantitative methods that can illuminate the process and impact of in-service education and training programs. There are quantitative methods of inquiry that can be integrated with case studies to form singular, comprehensive investigations of in-service education and training. Process/product evaluation and other traditional evaluation methods borrowed from curriculum evaluations (such as formative and summative) are insensitive to the challenges of evaluating in-service education and training. Thus, the essence of this reality that a methodology needs to be chosen is that a) there are many appropriate methods available and b) the best of traditional approaches to evaluating curriculum reform may not be applicable."

Fox considers that discussions about the need to involve teachers and others in evaluation decisions are best carried out in relation to specific tasks. Some issues, he observes, are general, such as the need to address the participating educators as adults and career professionals when evaluating the effectiveness of the in-service education and training on their own performance. Problems in dealing with traditional, organisationally supported, uneven power relationships also is shared across many contexts. Other issues are very context-bound such as the differing interpretations of who are the participating educators or who are the beneficiaries of the in-service education and training. Likewise, the discrepancies in evaluation experience between the chosen participants in the evaluation may be more or less significant depending upon the purpose of the in-service education and training programme.

Finally, drawing on his own experience of an unsuccessful attempt to give advice on evaluation, Fox focuses his recommendations on ways of promoting a fruitful dialogue between INSET policymakers, programme designers and evaluators, rather than on particular methodologies. He suggests that each group should explicitly seek to examine the contextual factors related to the evaluation task in hand, should question some specified assumptions about evaluation and should consider certain issues as a basis for a discussion about the viability and usefulness of a particular evaluation design. Although the national case studies contained accounts of particular evaluation methodologies, their brevity prevented them from being sufficiently context-rooted. Subsequent, detailed discussions between the evaluation teams from Swedish and British projects occurred as part of the co-development phase of the programme and fully supported Fox's contention that such discussions are more meaningful and useful when rooted in particular contextual settings.

Fox's argument that priority should be given to promoting and facilitating such dialogues between INSET policy makers, programme designers and evaluators is a convincing one. In this context, it is worth referring back to the interim reports which identified several types of evaluation target or focus (policy, programmes, activities) at various levels - national, local, institutional and individual. Discussion here has concentrated on the evaluation of programmes and activities at institutional level, but the issues and recommendations have equal relevance to the other targets and levels. Thus, evaluations or reviews of INSET policy at, say, local authority level ought to be the subject of a dialogue of the kind described by Fox.

INSET evaluation can be, and is being, carried out by a whole range of practitioners - teachers, professional tutors (or their equivalents), lecturers, INSET co-ordinators, advisers, inspectors, professional associations and INSET committees at school, college, local authority and national levels. Given the likely growth of INSET in the medium and long term and the need to evaluate INSET now and in the future, it is abundantly clear that it would take an army of outside researchers to do the job; it is equally clear that this would be a totally impractical solution.

Although finance and logistics dictate that self-monitoring and self-evaluation of INSET are likely to predominate, we should also recognise that these are, in any case, desirable activities for a profession. If effective self-evaluation is to be carried out then three main steps must be taken. First, the appropriateness of the formal self-evaluation agents and procedures (e.g. the appointment of professional tutors, local education authority co-ordinators and the setting up of units and committees) should be reviewed at each system level - school, providing agency, local and national. Second, relatively simple and easy-to-use self-evaluation procedures should be developed: these will need to build upon existing practice in schools, colleges and local authorities and be further refined by drawing upon the methods of professional researchers. See Steadman (112) for a helpful review. Third, key people like professional tutors and INSET co-ordinators in colleges and LEAs should be given the opportunity to attend short practical evaluation training courses.

Many of the problems and issues outlined here will only be serious ones for the professional researcher working on contract to evaluate INSET programmes and policies. Funding bodies need to be aware of these problems, too, and need to recognise their implication for the contract and the subsequent implementation of the research design. Researchers need to consider carefully the implications of adopting and advocating one particular style of evaluation: specifically they should beware of an exclusive adoption of process evaluations and equating these, simplistically, with illuminative evaluation. Recent experience both in the United States and in the United Kingdom suggests strongly that a pluralistic evaluation strategy, in which a variety of disciplines and techniques - both qualitative and quantitative - are employed, may well be feasible and more productive - both practically and theoretically.

Two main prerequisites are necessary if pluralistic strategies are to be adopted. First, researchers must be equipped through their training and experience to decide what approach is appropriate for a particular task. Second, national funding bodies and research agencies must be prepared both to use larger, multi-disciplinary research teams for appropriate tasks and to look to the career and training needs of researchers. In addition, professional researchers should acknowledge an obligation to contribute to the development of the evaluation guidelines for INSET providers suggested above.

VIII. EFFECTIVE INSET

Most of the research and evaluation work on INSET has been done in the United States and it is salutary to note Howey's (85) remark that there has been little rigorous review of it. Similarly, in a recent paper on the same topic, Yarger and Galluzzo (120) argue that the language and terms used to describe programmes and activities (e.g. "workshops" and "consultancy") are so imprecise that "research on in-service education has no standards for comparison" and that therefore "we know far less than we think we know" about effective INSET. Another new paper (75), by T.B. Greenfield, a Canadian, gives a sombre warning about the lack of impact made by research, theory and, by extension, training, upon the behaviour of education administrators. He might equally well have been talking about the impact of INSET in general in most Member countries.

Some progress has, however, been made. Batten (47) has reported on an extensive evaluation of the Australian School Commission's Development Program. She concluded that no one model has emerged to demonstrate the best way to achieve effective professional development. She also stressed the importance of teacher involvement in course planning and follow-up work and said that "No single aspect of the Program has been received with such universal acclaim as the trends towards school-centred professional development."

Evidence about effective INSET is also arising in related fields. A notable and influential example is the series of studies into the process of change at the school level carried out by the Rand Corporation. McLaughlin and Marsh (99) summarise their implications for staff development as follows:

"In summary the Rand study suggests that effective staff-development activities should incorporate five general assumptions about professional learning:

- Teachers possess important clinical expertise.
- Professional learning is an adaptive and heuristic process.

- Professional learning is a long-term, non-linear process.
- Professional learning must be tied to school-site program-building efforts.
- Professional learning is critically influenced by organisational factors in the school site and in the district.

These assumptions support a view of staff development emphasizing learning for professionals as part of program building in an organisational context."

Given that importance is being attached to school-focused INSET, it is surprising that more use has not been made of organisation development as a strategy for improving the school as a problem-solving system - see Schmuck (110) and Mulford (32). One explanation is that it requires a high degree of specific technical experience and competence on the part of the trainers. Nevertheless, in a comprehensive and critical review of organisation development practices in the United States and Canada, Fullan et al (70) state that "it appears to be a good way to increase instructional innovation, increase participation by all levels of personnel and to improve various aspects of task and socio-emotional functioning, if it is done <u>right</u>!"

Following a review of research relevant to school-focused INSET, Fullan (17) concluded:

"Finally, virtually all studies of needs have indicated that lack of time and energy for participating in professional development is a fundamental barrier to success.
It would be pointless to cite numerous other studies which have resulted in similar findings. A more interesting question is what does all of this tell us about effective in-service. If we are not careful, the answer will be 'deceptively little'. We know that most current in-service work is ineffective because it is frequently based on single-shot workshops involving large or in any case undifferentiated groups of teachers, provides limited time for teachers to learn, has little evaluation or practical follow-up support, and is not linked to particular classroom or school problems. Correspondingly, we also know that the majority of teachers desire more in-service activities, if they can participate in identifying the objectives, and in planning and choosing in-service activities; if the program focus is practical and classroom/school specific; if fellow teachers and local consultants are used as resource people; if the conditions (e.g. time) are conducive to learning;

and if there is some direct follow-up and support for facilitating the application of what is learned."

In a frequently quoted review of evaluation findings in this field, Lawrence (96) considered 97 studies and came to some provisional conclusions about effective INSET. He concluded that school-based INSET was more effective in influencing complex behaviour changes and teacher attitudes; that the collaborative involvement of teachers in course planning led to greater success; that it was easier to achieve success in improving teacher rather than pupil performance, in changing teacher behaviour rather than attitudes and, finally, in improving teachers' knowledge rather than behaviour.

Nevertheless, the Lawrence study has been criticised by Nicholson et al (103) as being "rather primitive scientifically" and has been subjected to detailed critical analysis by Cruikshank et al (60) who concluded that, because of its reporting and methodological shortcomings, the study's conclusions "must be considered as hunches or reasonable hypotheses". They go on to suggest a way forward for research on INSET which assumes that it is only a special case of teaching research. The complexities and difficulties of researching teacher effectiveness are well known so they are rightly cautious in the claim they make for their suggested approach.

Essentially, they advocate that INSET research should be more context specific and certainly this is in line with other contemporary thinking. One of the main virtues of the Lawrence study is that it highlighted the need to ask "effective for what?" and that some methods will be effective for achieving some aims in some circumstances but not in others. Similarly, Feiman-Nemser and Floden (69) argue that different models of teacher development are based upon assumptions about what kind of INSET is effective; for example those associated with teachers' centres believe that INSET is more effective if it offers warmth, concreteness, time and the opportunity to think.

In a particularly relevant and interesting study, Joyce and Showers (91) distinguish between two purposes of INSET: the "fine tuning" of existing skills and the learning of new skills. Each brings different problems, but they argue, "fine tuning" is generally easier to achieve. They also distinguish between four levels of impact of training and five components of training. This enables them to formulate the question: "In the body of research on training, how much does each kind of training component appear to contribute to each level of impact?"

The four levels of impact are: awareness, the acquisition of concepts and organised knowledge, the learning of principles and skills and, finally, their application to problem-solving in the classroom. Joyce and Showers argue that it is only when the fourth level is reached that it is reasonable to look for impact on pupil learning. Their five components of training are:

1. Presentation of theory or description of skill or strategy.
2. Modelling or demonstration of skills or models of teaching.
3. Practice in simulated and classroom settings.
4. Structured and open-ended feedback (provision of information about performance).
5. Coaching for application (hands-on, in-classroom assistance with the transfer of skills and strategies to the classroom).

Joyce and Showers summarise their findings as follows:

"For maximum effectiveness of most in-service activities, it appears wisest to include several and perhaps all of the training components we have listed (see, for example; Orme, 1966). Where the fine tuning of style is the focus, modelling, practice under simulated conditions, and practice in the classroom, combined with feedback, will probably result in considerable changes. Where the mastery of a new approach is the desired outcome, presentations and discussions of theory and coaching to application are probably necessary as well. If the theory of a new approach is well presented, the approach is demonstrated, practice is provided under simulated conditions with careful and consistent feedback, and that practice is followed by application in the classroom with coaching and further feedback, it is likely that the vast majority of teachers will be able to expand their repertoire to the point where they can utilize a wide variety of approaches to teaching and curriculum.

If any of these components are left out, the impact of training will be weakened in the sense that fewer numbers of people will progress to the transfer level (which is the only level that has significant meaning for school improvement). The most effective training activities, then, will be those that combine theory, modelling, practice, feedback and coaching to application. The knowledge base seems firm enough that we can predict that if those components are in fact combined in in-service programs, we can expect the outcomes to be considerable at all levels."

The implications of these findings, which they offer as reasonable hypotheses, for the three main types of INSET described earlier, are considerable. The universities and colleges that provide long courses of the award-bearing type might well argue that they are concerned with education and the teaching of knowledge rather than skills.

Those agencies offering shorter courses of a job-related kind and those who advocate school-focused or on-the-job training may well have cause to reflect that their present offerings are neither long enough, comprehensive enough nor coherent enough to achieve the purposes they set themselves. Joyce and Showers' conclusions are indeed a sharp and salutary reminder that INSET which aims to improve the complex business of teaching and learning can only be effective if it is relatively lengthy, labour intensive and, therefore, expensive.

IX. <u>MAIN CONCLUSIONS AND
THEIR IMPLICATIONS FOR POLICY AND RESEARCH</u>

In the foregoing synthesis of studies, enquiries and experimentation carried out over the last five years we have attempted to fulfil the primary purpose of the INSET project by putting policy makers and those who influence them, at all functional levels, in a position to extract from the experiences of colleagues abroad those ideas and practices that, suitably adapted, could help them to improve INSET in their own countries. It now remains to consider what general conclusions may additionally be drawn from this body of informational material and from the deliberations at the final Intergovernmental Conference. Here we shall have a special eye on implications for national education policies and programmes for research.

A. TEACHERS: NEEDS, PARTICIPATION AND INCENTIVES

The follow-up activity on teachers as adult learners ("Adult Learning and Development") has confirmed that this is an extremely important aspect of the needs of teachers for INSET. However, it revealed that participating countries had few substantial research findings to offer that could be easily adapted or used in improving in-service programmes in this respect. There is clearly room, therefore, for considerably more research and development work in the countries interested in this field. In the course of this, much might be learned from a more directly comparative study of adult education and training in other professions (for example, in medicine, engineering and social work) since preliminary indications are that several of the tasks and problems are similar and that some of the solutions may be generalisable to teacher education.

Although career profiles and other general needs analysis instruments have their uses, country studies reveal that more context-specific approaches should be developed. There is general agreement, for example, that beginning teachers and, at the other end of the experience scale, principals, both have their particular in-service needs. What is lacking are simple and short methods of analysing the different aspects of their jobs for in-service purposes. Probationers' classroom management and pedagogical skills can be distinguished from their knowledge of their particular specialist subject: each will generate context-specific needs. Similarly, the principal's staff leadership and office management functions generate different INSET needs.

At this point an important paradox is worth emphasizing. Throughout the many conferences, seminars and reports there was a recurring plea for INSET to be rooted in practice, to be relevant, to be context-specific and for theory to be based upon an analysis of practice. One apparently logical response to teachers who say this is to suggest that the needs analysis and training support should both take place _inside_ their classrooms, but this is usually rejected as being too threatening and even unprofessional. Yet if the principal and ultimate goal of INSET is to improve pupils' learning and if Joyce and Showers' conclusions (as already summarised) are valid, then it is surely inescapable that professionally acceptable ways of providing classroom-based INSET have got to be devised.

The task of needs identification inevitably raises the questions: how should it be done and who should do it? These were not directly addressed in the project but the evidence from research in several countries indicates that the process of making a satisfactory diagnosis is a lengthy and time-consuming one - see Baker (46) and Hite and McIntyre (83). There is also general agreement amongst practitioners that INSET needs can be more effectively and validly identified if the teachers involved participate collaboratively in the process. Indeed, there is widespread agreement that more effective INSET can be achieved if the participating teachers can contribute collaboratively to decisions about general INSET policies and programmes at all stages - planning, implementation, evaluation and follow-up. Thus procedures are needed at several levels:

1. an individual teacher, in consultation with a school-based professional tutor, a department head, and the principal, and within a school policy framework;
2. the department or functional group, in consultation with a professional tutor, the principal and the school's professional development committee;
3. the school, in consultation with local external advisers and the local consultative group on INSET, on which teachers and providers are represented;

4. area groups of schools, in consultation with local advisers and consultative groups;
5. the local authority, in consultation with its own consultative groups;
6. at national level, the government in consultation with its national consultative group;
7. the providing agency, in consultation with a consultative group;
8. the programme and course organisers, in consultation with the participants.

A key policy issue is whether non-professionals are represented at any of these levels and stages. What of non-teaching staff, parents and other community representatives for example? And what of pupils?

One of the most controversial aspects of INSET needs concerns the feasibility and desirability of offering extrinsic incentives for INSET. Inevitably the question of incentives was bound up with the question of certification for INSET courses. Three broad types of course seem to take place in Member countries. Type a) courses are those which are neither certificated nor linked directly to promotion or increased salary. Type b) courses are those that are certificated but still not directly linked to promotion or salary increases. Type c) courses are those that are both certificated and linked directly to promotion and/or salary increases. It was clear that many participants at the Intergovernmental Conference regarded an undue emphasis on Type c) as counter-productive and undesirable since it could lead to the seeking of certificates for the wrong reasons.

There can be no general agreement as to whether INSET should be regarded as a compulsory duty, whether it should be a right for all teachers, whether it should be offered in school time or not and whether it should be financed wholly or exclusively by the individual teacher or the employing authority. Important and relevant as these questions are to the incentives issue, they have to be asked and answered in the context of specific conditions within any one country.

B. SCHOOL NEEDS AND PROGRAMMES

The general feasibility and popularity of school-focused approaches to in-service have been well demonstrated in the course of the project. The strategy has received virtually unanimous approbation because of the way in which it attacks problems of relevance and significance for teachers, schools and community alike and because it can apparently act as a potent energising strategy for innovation and improvement without making excessive demands upon resources.

That being said, several words of caution are necessary. "School-focused" is still a relatively untried strategy: rather few examples were reported in the case studies. The available evidence also indicates that effective school-focused INSET requires authorities to devolve more autonomy to schools: several professional association representatives at the Conference pointed out that school-focused INSET could strengthen and reinforce systems which were already highly centralised and would therefore be unacceptable to many teachers. They also argued that school-focused INSET should be in no way seen as excluding other forms of INSET. Although this does not seem to have been intended by its advocates, the point was nevertheless well taken: it is vitally important that existing methods and approaches (for example, the advanced degree courses at universities) should be maintained and developed.

The Conference paid particular attention to the question: What is meant by the school? Normally it is assumed that a school staff consists of the professional teachers and administrators. It follows that school-focused INSET would adopt a straightforward linear process: self-evaluation by individuals and groups and the assumption that this would in turn lead to the improvement of curriculum and instruction. However, there are, of course, many obstacles to the improvement of schools and of pupil learning. Many, if not most, of these obstacles are quite outside the control of professional teachers. Obstacles like inadequate buildings, poor facilities, poor pupil attitudes and a sceptical community all impinge upon the educational process, yet their improvement and the money that is very often needed to carry out such improvements, are all beyond the direct influence of teachers. If school-focused INSET simply involves teachers it is bound to ignore this important reality. It follows that for certain purposes it is necessary to extend the definition of a school staff to include non-professional workers in the school – cleaners, secretarial staff, etc., and of course parents and community representatives. Experience in certain Member countries, for example Sweden, demonstrates that this can be a powerful means of bringing about greater mutual understanding between the various groups and also of strengthening the likelihood that school and instructional improvement can be brought about more effectively.

Whatever the composition of the "target group", there was general agreement that effective school-focused INSET requires a sound, well-integrated external support structure which itself depends upon the development of new and flexible partnership between INSET agencies like inspectors and higher education institutions. Within schools, careful planning and organisational arrangements appear to be crucial to the success of the approach.

C. TRAINERS AND THEIR TRAINING NEEDS

Advisers and inspectors play varying INSET roles in Member countries. For example, in the United Kingdom they are extremely active, whereas in the Netherlands their role in INSET appears to be minimal. It is surely important for all countries to consider whether or not it is a sensible use of such personnel resources for inspectors to concentrate on their inspectorial role in preference to the advisory or INSET role, or whether some mixture of the two can co-exist happily. Alternatives should also be actively considered and reviewed. In particular, it seems clear that advisory teachers on short-term release from schools can act as effective INSET agents but, as the Australian evidence demonstrates, the way in which they work and the targets which they set for themselves can be of crucial importance in determining their effectiveness. Because of their potential, however, it would seem sensible to carry out systematic study of advisory teachers.

Within schools, the evidence about school-based teacher educator roles is somewhat ambiguous. For example, although the professional tutor role has been widely publicised in the United Kingdom, it is far from clear that it is actually being implemented in many schools or that it has been well received by teachers. This is especially true in primary schools: but even in secondary schools, the role as originally envisaged does not appear to be a feasible one. However, what does seem to be practical is to define the tasks of staff development within specific schools and then to identify people in those schools to carry them out. Thus, in British secondary schools, deputy heads appear to be well suited for this job whereas, in primary schools, the head, perhaps working in association with an external advisory teacher, appears to be the most appropriate person. Solutions to this problem will necessarily be country and context specific and the internal factors that influence them should be the focus of more detailed study locally. During the Conference, stress was given to the value of using peers, that is other teachers, as trainers at school level.

In clarifying the kind of training that various INSET trainers should receive, the following procedure seemed to work best. The first step is to identify clearly the people who carry out training roles and then to analyse those roles and consider the contextual factors that affect them. The next step is to define the main tasks of the INSET trainers, to identify their main clients and to consider what knowledge, skills and attitudes the trainers need to carry out those tasks for those clients in the particular setting in which they work. Finally, the implications of these answers for any training-the-trainers programmes should be decided. At present, the training of trainers continues to be an unclear, under-financed and under-studied area in all Member countries.

D. TRAINING METHODS, MATERIALS AND CONTENT

Further work on the training of trainers should be closely linked with a study of training materials. It is important here to learn the lessons of previous experience, particularly in the United States. The Synthesis Report on training the trainers stresses that methods and materials should clearly indicate the context and the purposes for which they were designed and should indicate ways in which they may be modified for differing contexts and purposes. The validity of this approach is confirmed by recent work which argues the need to ensure that curriculum materials have the possibility for local adaptation built in to their design and presentation. This characteristic of "adaptability" is one that is equally relevant to training-the-trainers materials both within and between countries. In other words, in considering the implications and possible value of materials beyond the boundaries of any one area or country, the ways in which they might be adapted should be made explicit from the outset.

The potentially vast and diffuse topic of the content of INSET was not directly or separately addressed during the project. Rather, a study was made of the principal factors that influence its selection. These include the general purposes of INSET, teachers' characteristics and needs, incentives and participation mechanisms and the immediate needs of the school and wider system, for example brought about by declining enrolments.

The importance of constructing programmes which take account of the needs of teachers as adult workers was stressed throughout the Conference. In this context it is worth looking at the way in which activities and programmes that are designed for individual professional and career development actually work. A great deal of money and time is spent, for instance, on award-bearing courses at universities and other institutions of higher education. It is surely important to ask how and in what ways they are effective. Moreover, if career development is an important aim of INSET, the position of women in the profession is worthy of serious study: evidence from several countries indicates that they are seriously under-represented at higher levels in the profession and it would be worth looking for ways, if any, in which INSET could help to rectify this situation.

Three further general issues are worth raising. The concept of a continuum of professional education – for example, the so-called triple-I model of initial, induction and in-service - attracted considerable support: clearly, the concept has profound consequences for the content of the three stages but quite what these are is far from clear. The concept of content based upon an analysis of action rather than on apparently abstract theory, upon knowledge for action rather than knowledge for understanding, also attracted support, but the ways in which such a philosophy could successfully be put into effect are also obscure. The third issue is related to both of these and it concerns the nature of professional knowledge. Teachers aspire to professional status in most Member countries and, if it is accepted that one mark of a profession is that it bases its practice upon a distinctive and coherent body of knowledge and theory, then it follows that teachers should be able to delineate such a body of knowledge: the evidence from the project is that this is not possible, at least at present. The implications of all three of these issues surely deserve further study.

E. EXTERNAL SUPPORT STRUCTURES

The first task for the participants in the Conference who were discussing this topic was to clarify some of the terms involved. A notable example was that of the term "teachers' centre". A quick check revealed that, in many countries, teachers' centres do not exist in any recognisable form and that even where they do exist, they differ considerably. Moreover, different trends are clear: in Italy they are emerging: in the United Kingdom many have been closed; in the United States the numbers are expanding and in Australia they are more likely to involve the community. The School-Focused study had confirmed that teachers' centres differ considerably both between and within countries. They can act as the base and focal point for school-focused strategies but it does not necessarily follow that this will be the case. Teachers' centres, like other external agencies, have to be analysed and costed in order to assess their actual and potential effectiveness in this and other INSET approaches.

If various component parts of the external support structure are to be used to the greatest effect, then it would seem sensible to try to reach agreement, at least within each Member country, about certain guiding principles. The Dutch experience provided useful guidelines. They decided that the first question to ask was "What kind of school do we need?" Only then were they prepared to ask the question, "What kind of support structure do we need to achieve such schools?" A development of this approach could involve asking the question "How much contact does an individual teacher need with external support agencies?" Let us suppose that any one teacher should have at least one hour's contact per term with a visiting external adviser (whether it be a local inspector/adviser or an expert from a pedagogic centre). Three hours per year would then be the minimum and it would follow that, having made due allowance for the differences between urban and rural settings, we could calculate the number of such advisers that were needed in any particular area. Such an approach is surely worth exploring in Member countries.

The extent to which institutions of higher education act as INSET providing agencies varies between countries. However, if they are to be effectively used, then it seems clear from evidence from Australia, the United Kingdom and the United States that their internal structure and the way in which staff incentives are structured in relation to the more traditional courses would have to be reviewed. If such institutions are to engage in part-time in-service, then the way in which part-time students are valued and financed within the institution is of crucial importance. If staff are to engage in school-focused INSET, then the way in which consultancy activities are valued must also be reviewed. The extent to which such institutions are required to specialise in conventional longer, award-bearing courses will undoubtedly affect the answers to these questions. At present, for example, there are few incentives for college staff in the United States and the United Kingdom to adopt new and imaginative approaches; they gain more career rewards by sustaining and extending traditional courses.

F. EVALUATION, COSTS, FINANCE AND RESOURCE UTILIZATION

At the Conference, a very simple and convincing answer was given to the question "Why should we cost and evaluate in-service?": expenditure had to be justified both locally and nationally, and priorities had to be set to decide whether more or less should be spent on one form of in-service compared with another and on in-service as compared with, let us say, the social services; cost and evaluation data could help in establishing these priorities. It was, therefore, salutary to hear the conclusion reached by the national representatives that it will rarely be possible to obtain evaluation data which tells us about the effect of INSET on pupil learning. It seems, therefore, that (as in other aspects of social policy) decisions about priorities have to be taken, and will continue to have to be taken, in the light of information that is incomplete.

According to the evidence of the reports, a great deal of knowledge now exists about evaluation and about the appropriateness of particular methods in particular contexts. The problem identified in the Synthesis Report was that this knowledge is not being used properly by planners, policy makers, INSET organisers and evaluators. The solution offered was that these interested parties should hold detailed and systematic discussions about the possibilities and limitations of a particular evaluation design before, during and after its implementation. In addition, it continues to be important that researchers should be adequately trained in a wide range of techniques and that teachers and others involved should collaborate in the evaluation from the outset.

The work on costing in-service has proved instructive and in many respects the overall conclusions must be similar to those reached about adult learning: although much useful work has been completed, many of the concepts are unclear and there is an urgent need for further intensive and systematic study. Costs are of such fundamental importance that it is doubly surprising to discover the haziness which exists in all Member countries about the whole issue. At the Conference two main reasons were suggested: the lack of agreed nomenclature and definitions for INSET activities leads to unreliable cost analysis and the many and varied providing agencies often adopt different costing and financing arrangements. Thus, an apparently simple request for INSET costs to be calculated as a percentage of the total education budget cannot be met in most Member countries. This deficiency is a double-edged sword for neither can a precise answer be given to the question, "What are the costs of not providing INSET support for a new policy or an innovation?"

Underlying many complex financial questions are the basic ones of who does and should pay for INSET in terms of both money and time. Several of the reports had revealed that a great deal, and very often most, of the in-service in Member countries took place in the teachers' own time although it should be said that, by its very nature, this kind of information is difficult to obtain in a reliable form. From the teacher's point of view it seems essential that adequate release time should be given as an entitlement for INSET. On the other hand, community and business interests stress that there is no reason for teachers to obtain further qualifications and advancement at public expense. During the Intergovernmental Conference some participants expressed the view that INSET made necessary by changes in national or local policy should be paid for by the State, whereas INSET aimed at the individual teacher's career development or personal education should not - but this was by no means a unanimous view.

Many financial questions can only be answered in the specific context of each country's circumstances. The question of whether INSET should take place in employers' time, for example, is bound up with the broader question of teachers' contracts and conditions of service. Similarly, where INSET is viewed as a national rather than a local responsibility, the costs may be pooled and paid for collectively.

However, much can be learned from the mechanisms that Member countries have devised to achieve maximum value for money from their available INSET resources. Participants cited the following examples: establishing voluntary liaison organisations, at local and national levels, with representatives from teachers, parents, higher education, education authorities, business, industry, etc. to strengthen the "horizontal" co-ordination of external support for schools; establishing "leagues" of school and "networks" of individual teachers or principals working on similar innovations; reviewing the roles of certain agencies like the inspectorate and the teacher training institutions to establish whether they can make a more substantial contribution to INSET; encouraging schools to mount their own INSET programmes by giving them an INSET budget and allowing them to "bank" staff replacement hours; strengthening the vertical co-ordination of INSET by establishing local and national organisations to co-ordinate initial, induction and in-service education and training.

G. GENERAL POLICY CONSIDERATIONS

The central focus of the project has necessarily been upon the technical and operational aspects of INSET, but those involved have been constantly reminded of the essentially political context within which INSET has to operate by two factors: the steady deterioration in the economic climate and the growing impact of a declining birth rate. They provide the background against which all discussions about INSET and the improvement of schools must take place: but, profoundly constraining as they undoubtedly are, they should not prevent serious consideration being given to what can still be achieved. Whatever the immediate circumstances, INSET policy will continue to be important at all system levels as a means of maintaining and improving schooling within Member countries.

Both the Adult Learning and School-Focused enquiries have pointed to a common difficulty - that of achieving sustained and continuing change. The evidence from studies of innovations for individuals, groups and organisations like schools and local authorities is that they all require extremely careful planning, appropriate resources and a well-thought-through implementation strategy over a lengthy period of time. Research cited in Section VIII, for example, concludes that changes in teachers' behaviour can only be accomplished if all five stages of a lengthy and costly process are carried out, and that effective school change can only take place if a number of conditions, all difficult to achieve, exist. So, desirable as speedy and inexpensive changes undoubtedly are from a political and economic viewpoint, they are not likely to be easily attained, and strategies for change which assume otherwise are not likely to prove cost effective in the long run. The implications of these findings are clearly worthy of further study, not least to test out their validity in differing national contexts.

The critical impact of these differing national contexts should not be under-estimated. During the course of the project, the following factors were identified as having an important bearing upon the way INSET was provided and perceived in each country: the degree of centralised curriculum control and how much discretion is allowed to teachers for curriculum development; whether or not teachers are government employees or civil servants and what this implies for their conditions of service; the normal length of the teaching day, week and year; whether the career structure was high or flat and specifically whether or not middle management or leadership positions (e.g. heads of subject departments) exist; the amount of discretion granted to principals over salaries and promotion within a school (e.g. heads' use of a points system); the amount of teacher participation which already takes place in, for example, the governance of teacher education.

In the context of this particular project and of the present report, participating countries might find it useful to consider the extent to which they now regard INSET as embracing the five Purposes distinguished in Diagram 1 in Section II. The following more specific policy questions can also be generated from a consideration of these Purposes:

- Who is seen as the main beneficiary of any particular INSET programme or activity - the teacher (Purposes 3, 4 and 5) or the school (Purposes 1 and 2)?
- Who actually does and should provide any particular type of INSET? For example, is INSET aimed mainly at professional knowledge for understanding (Purpose 4) best located in institutions of higher education?
- Whose time actually is, and should be, spent on any particular type of INSET? For example, should INSET aimed mainly at system development (Purposes 1 and 2) take place exclusively or primarily in employer or school time, and should INSET aimed mainly

at individual development (Purposes 3, 4 and 5) take place primarily or exclusively in the teacher's own time?
- Who actually does and should pay the attendance fees and expenses for different types of INSET? For example, should the employer cover all fees and expenses for INSET aimed mainly at system development (Purposes 1 and 2) and should the teacher cover all fees and expenses aimed mainly at individual development (Purposes 3, 4 and 5)?
- Do and should teachers engage in recurrent education of a non-vocational kind (Purpose 5)? If so, in whose time and at whose expense?
- In answering these questions, whose viewpoint is being adopted and would a change in this viewpoint lead to significantly different answers? If so, what are the implications of these differences?

It must be acknowledged that the distinction between individual and system needs is a simplistic one; but discussions about INSET are not helped by the existing multiplicity of definitions and purposes which (as we have already noted) apparently co-exist both within and between countries. The notion of the primary or main purpose of any particular INSET programme or activity is offered as a clarifying criterion which could be helpful in dealing with intractable issues relating to costs and conditions of service for teachers. For there is little doubt that the nature and purpose of INSET is itself central to the debate about the nature of teaching as a profession or semi-profession, and about the contractual obligations of teachers and their employing authorities. For instance, there is the basic question about how much teacher time and how much school or employer time (in the form of teacher release) is and should be given over to INSET. Associated with this are broader questions about what percentage of the teaching force actually is, and should ideally be, engaged in self-renewal activities, for instance on longer courses, at any one time. Is the British suggestion of 3 per cent generally acceptable? If so, why and on what criteria? Or is it arbitrary and culture-bound? What answers are given to similar questions in industry and in other professions?

An underlying issue turns upon the answer to the question as to whether teaching is and ought to be a profession or semi-profession. For example, in the American context, Broudy (57) argues that although competency-based teacher education (CBTE) methods are quite inappropriate for professionals, they are appropriate for para-professionals. Naturally, this is not a view that goes unchallenged but it does offer one way of analysing the vexed question of the content of INSET.

A related question concerns the roles of professional associations in INSET. The position appears to vary considerably from country to country; for example, in some countries, professional subject associations seem to be very active in INSET and so, too, do teacher unions; in others, this appears to be less true. This is clearly an aspect of INSET provision which is worth further systematic study, bearing as it does upon important professional issues about the content, governance and finance of INSET. In such a study, wider political considerations should be given due attention. In certain Member countries, several professions, notably the medical profession, exercise control over entry standards, training content and certification, and steps have also been taken, for example in Scotland, to establish General Teaching Councils with similar powers. This aspect of INSET has been noticeably neglected in the project.

We may reasonably conclude that the ways in which INSET can meet the needs of the system, whether at school, local or national levels, are being very actively considered in participating countries. Teachers, principals, advisers, administrators and researchers are all agreed that school-focused INSET is better received and more effective than the traditional course-based model. Indeed, in some Member countries (e.g. in Sweden and California) INSET is being used consciously and deliberately as an instrument of social policy. Other evidence to support this comes from the Netherlands where INSET is being seen as a major part of a proposed strategy for increasing the relative autonomy and problem-solving capacity of secondary schools.

This shift in emphasis raises several policy issues. In considering plans and priorities, organisers need to be realistic in their publicly stated expectations and goals for INSET, not least because the wider community and its politicians are frequently unrealistic about such matters. INSET is no panacea. It cannot make much impact on those fundamental social, cultural, political and economic constraints within which schools and teachers have to operate. Goals have to be formulated with caution. Moreover, desirable as it certainly is to meet the needs of schools and the wider needs of society, the needs of individual teachers must be kept very clearly in mind. A balance has to be struck which ensures that the legitimate aspirations of individual teachers for career development and further personal education are met. Hence, appropriate funding for advanced studies at university and for sabbatical periods must be maintained and extended.

Two further policy issues are highlighted by this shift in emphasis. The Dutch and Swedish experience raises the first very directly: to what extent do Member countries consider it desirable and feasible to relate INSET policy and programmes to the promotion of a particular concept of the school? The second is raised by the British concept, not in fact implemented, of the "triple-I continuum" (initial, induction and in-service) of teacher education and training. Among others, Belbenoit (3) advocates the adoption of this guiding philosophical concept, but it is far from clear what it actually means in practice or how it could be achieved.

H. PRIORITIES FOR RESEARCH AND DEVELOPMENT

Perhaps the first and most important conclusion to be drawn from the impressive surveys of practice and research contributed to the project by Member countries is that far from enough is generally known about effective in-service and effective school improvement. Contemporary economic pressures should not be allowed to obscure this simple fact.

In particular, it is clear that the burgeoning interest and activity in INSET is, to a worrying extent, built upon an act of faith. Expenditure on research into INSET has been minimal, so it is hardly surprising that we have so little systematic and reliable information about costs, resource use, and effectiveness, both of particular approaches and overall investment. Undoubtedly the position has improved, but a great deal of research must be funded and carried out in individual countries if this situation is to be fully rectified.

No doubt each country will formulate its own categories and priorities. The categories used in Phase 2 of this project have considerable practical utility, while the models in the Interim Report, Table 2 and Appendix 3, offer a comprehensive analytic conceptual tool; both could well form the starting point for a national discussion of research and development priorities. Hall (77) has produced an excellent rationale and agenda for such a programme in an American context, while Yarger and Galluzzo's 1980 matrix (120) provides a valuable method for identifying the characteristics of quality research in INSET. In an OECD context, the feasibility of further sharing of international experience and research deserves close attention as a separate problem.

Accordingly, in view of the participants in the present project, it would seem sensible to build upon the work on INSET that has already been done by OECD CERI, developing it to meet the needs of Member countries during the 1980s. Several major substantive demands, tasks, constraints and problems from which such needs will arise have already been identified in Section II. To them one could add several more:

i) growing demands for teacher involvement in school decision-making;

ii) the problems of sustaining the job satisfaction and professional development of teachers in a period of contraction or no-growth and minimal promotion prospects;

iii) the problems of sustaining school improvement when resources are being cut and the general climate is not supportive of innovation;

iv) the introduction at the school level of computer facilities as aids to the storing, processing and utilisation of data for management purposes and of computing courses and computer appreciation throughout the curriculum;

v) the introduction or continuance of curriculum guidelines to ensure that all pupils experience some "common core" curricular experiences;

vi) increasing community/political demands for the introduction, continuance or strengthening of contracts which specify teachers' conditions of service in detail.

In order to make a relevant contribution to the resolution of such problems, two principal thrusts for future work are suggested here, both deriving from the two-fold purpose of INSET identified earlier: the career and professional development of individual teachers and the development of the school or the wider educational system but with the parameters of both being extended among the following lines.

Continuing Professional Education (Co.P.Ed.)

The earlier focus on the ways in which INSET meets the professional and career needs of individual teachers should be extended to embrace the initial and induction, as well as the in-service stages, thus rooting teacher education firmly in a recurrent or continuing education perspective. Although it is important that process issues of the kind considered in this report continue to be studied, probably this could best be done alongside analyses of immediate "substantive" educational problems like those listed above. Thus, Co.P.Ed. process issues would be studied in relation to topics like the management of contraction and the transition from school to work.

Within this framework, certain key process topics warrant further study, notably:

i) work completed or projected on the induction phase, e.g. in Australia, the United Kingdom, the United States, New Zealand, the Netherlands and Ireland;

ii) problems related to the articulation of the content of the initial, induction and in-service phases of Co.P.Ed.;
iii) successful methods in Co.P.Ed. especially those used for face-to-face, individualised training;
iv) the application of recent research on effective individual adult learning and effective organisational change;
v) the implications of related experience and practice in the continuing education of other professionals like social workers, doctors, engineers and industrial managers;
vi) evaluation, costing and financing of Co.P.Ed. with account being taken of relevant practice in other fields of recurrent education.

Management and Administration to strengthen the Problem-Solving Capacities of Schools

The earlier focus on the ways in which INSET can meet the development needs of schools and the wider system should be extended to embrace the totality of strategies needed to strengthen the problem-solving capacities of schools. This perspective draws particularly upon the school-focused studies undertaken in this project but also upon CERI's previous work on the creativity of the school (58) and upon subsequent research and experience in Member countries (54).

All of the substantive education problems listed above have two features in common; they raise issues and have consequences for the whole school and they cannot be dealt with by any one subject department or by an individual teacher. Alongside these systemic pressures and demands there are continuing pressures that impact directly upon subject departments and these, too, require a response and a reaction from schools.

The essence of the problem-solving perspective is that schools should be encouraged and enabled to adopt a pro-active, rather than a re-active approach to the maintenance and improvement of education standards. The practical relevance of these ideas is evident in several Member countries, including Sweden, Australia, the United Kingdom and the United States. A notable recent advocacy of these views occurred in the Netherlands where the "relatively autonomous" secondary school was seen as having the following characteristics:

"... the school is in a position to make its own educational policy, which enables it to make a conscious choice as to the sort of problem it wants to deal with. Potentially, the autonomous school has a greater problem-solving capacity than the other two types. By this we understand the extent to which the school, within a given framework, is able to create conditions in which:

- it can solve the practical problems which arise in the pursuit of its aims;
- it can take initiatives, design improvements, test them out and, if necessary, introduce those which are considered likely to further the aims pursued;
- it can adapt the internal organisation of the school in such a way as to facilitate the above-mentioned process;
- it can evaluate reforms developed by other bodies, examine their relevance for its own situation, adapt them if necessary, or reject them because they are not relevant to its policy;
- it can give educational answers to social developments which the school considers to be important." (116)

The differing political and administrative contexts within Member countries will, of course, significantly influence the extent to which these and similar ideas could be put into practice but even more limited versions of "autonomy" or "creativity" depend upon the existence of certain internal and external conditions. The focus of this suggested activity would be upon precisely what kind of internal school procedures and external conditions of support are needed if schools are to become effective problem-solvers in the 1980s.

More specifically, the central focus would be upon principals and senior staff in schools, for there is widespread agreement in most Member countries that the management and administrative skills of these senior staff are of crucial importance. Once again, studies would be considerably strengthened by relating them as directly as possible to substantive problems of the kind described earlier.

The following are examples of topics which could usefully be described and analysed within this framework.

   i) appropriate and effective leadership and management strategies for school heads and senior staff;
   ii) appropriate and effective in-service education and training to equip and support them in this approach;
   iii) appropriate and effective school decision-making procedures and internal organisational procedures and arrangements for systematic problem-solving, and the management of change;

iv) appropriate and effective staff appointments
       and procedures for curriculum development
       and implementation at the school level;
    v) appropriate and effective procedures for
       evaluating and costing the work of the
       school and for presenting an account to the
       community;
   vi) appropriate and effective external support,
       training and inspection arrangements;
  vii) appropriate and effective administrative
       and legal arrangements;
 viii) appropriate and effective budgetary and
       financing procedures.

X. A FRAMEWORK FOR THE DEVELOPMENT OF NEW POLICIES

Finally, in the light of a synthesis made by the OECD Secretariat of discussions in the various Intergovernmental Conference Working Groups and supporting documentation, the following precepts are offered as together providing a reasonable conceptual framework for use when policies for in-service education and training of teachers and strategies for educational change are being discussed.

   i) Schools must be capable at all times of responding in various ways to the differentiated and varied needs of their pupils and of society.
  ii) Whatever the characteristics of the new teaching and learning strategies being implemented, the functions, attitudes and qualifications of school personnel will continue to play a fundamental role.
 iii) Because of the above, and taking into account the decreasing recruitment of newly-trained teachers and the need to maintain, by all possible means, the internal dynamism of the teaching profession, in-service education and training for the various categories of school personnel remains a high priority in the coming years.
  iv) There is increasing complexity in the problems that confront each individual school, and which it must endeavour to solve under conditions of optimum freedom of action within its own surroundings. This implies that, more than in former times, training activities should centre on the school and its problems and that such activities should take an increasingly collaborative form. It also implies that related support structures need to be set up by the responsible authorities, based where appropriate on a clear legal basis, so as to complement and stimulate on a continuous basis the functions of the school in this field.
   v) In recent years, the difficulties in offering attractive education and training

programmes, in what concerns both objectives and methods and content, show that the personal and professional experience of the teachers, their motivations, their working environment - in short, their condition as workers - have not sufficiently been taken into consideration; and that those who are most directly concerned have not adequately participated in the decision-making process. There is general agreement that, as in other sectors of activity affected by new socio-economic conditions, the teachers must be able to benefit from a continuing training corresponding to their professional needs within the context of changing educational and social systems.

vi) As a consequence, one important development is the increasing stress upon directing INSET at meeting the needs of the school, of groups and individuals within the school. The term "school-focused" has been used to describe this approach. It is important, however, to recognise that the philosophy of that strategy must be interpreted as permeating different types of INSET; these other types of INSET (i.e. the longer award-bearing courses, courses for promotion, etc.) should also continue according to the priorities elaborated between the various partners concerned.

vii) It can be concluded that each member of the school personnel must be provided with an opportunity for consistent, integrated, personal and professional development throughout his/her career (where initial training would only be a starting point), enabling both his/her own training needs and those of the changing educational system to be met as closely as possible.

viii) Any INSET activity must include an evaluation device, the modalities of which, according to the complexity of implementation, would have to be discussed among the various partners. This evaluation might help decision-makers and practitioners choose the most appropriate training mechanisms; and, in training schemes centred more on the individual and the group, personal and collective self-evaluation will play an increasing role.

ix) The issue of costs and resources for training needs, moreover, must be considered in this context. In a difficult economic situation, rising costs involved in teacher replacement raise the thorny problem of how training costs should be met.

x) The impact of the economic and demographic trends on all the above issues results in a growing politicisation of the debate concerning the teaching profession and in particular its training context. It would be useful if all the partners concerned could agree to discuss these key issues as explicitly as possible, in terms of both objectives and means, and to this end strive for a consistent amelioration of the necessary qualitative and quantitative data.

XI. BIBLIOGRAPHY

A. THE OECD INSET PROJECT

Unpublished reports and documents prepared in the framework of the Project.

Phase 1

The following national reports, each containing detailed bibliographies, were made generally available as Gratis Documents in 1976 under the general title:

Innovation in In-Service Education and Training of Teachers

1. Australia : M. Skilbeck, G. Evans and J. Harvey

2. Canada : M. Belanger

3. France : G. Belbenoit

4. Germany/Switzerland : K. Frey, P. Posch, U. Kröll, J. Cavadini, U.P. Lattman, H. Fischer and K. Arregger

5. Japan : H. Azuma

6. Netherlands : N. Deen and E.S. Boeder-Rijdes

7. Sweden : S. Marklund and H. Eklund

8. United Kingdom : R. Bolam and J. Porter

9. United States : L. Rubin and K. Howey

10. Italy : M. Reguzzoni

11. Innovation in In-Service Education and Training of Teachers: Practice and Theory (R. Bolam), OECD/CERI, Paris, 1978 (referred to as the "Interim Report").

Phase 2

(Headings conform with the devolution of work as shown on the Structural Chart, p. 7)

Adult learning and development

12. Points of View Reflecting Experience in the United Kingdom (James Porter, with contributions by: Clem Adelman, Jack Chambers, L. John Chapman, John Elliott), 1979.

13. An American Point of View (Dean Corrigan, Martin Haberman, Kenneth Howey), 1979.

14. Issues and Practices in Adult Education: Some Points of Reference for Teacher Training (Gilles Ferry), 1979.

15. Synthesis Report (D. Corrigan), 1980.

School-focused training and teachers' centres

16. The Australian Experience (L. Ingvarson et al.), 1980.

17. The Canadian Experience (M. Fullan), 1980.

18. The New Zealand Experience (A. Forrest), 1980.

19. The United States Experience (K. Howey), 1980.

20. Teachers' Centres in Italy (M. Vicentini-Missoni), 1978.

21. Educational Guidance Services in the Netherlands (B. Groenhagen), 1978.

22. Teachers' Centres in the United Kingdom (A. Griggs with the assistance of J. Gregory), 1978.

23. Teachers' Centres in the United States (K. Devaney), 1978.

24. Teachers' Centres in Australia (B. Fallon), 1978.

25. Synthesis Report: School-focused In-service Education: Clarification of a new concept and strategy (K. Howey), 1980.

The evaluation of INSET

26. Three School-based Models for Conducting Follow-up of Teacher Education and Training (Gary D. Borich), 1978.

27. The Evaluation of INSET for Teachers in the United Kingdom (Colin McCabe), 1978.

28. The Evaluation of INSET for Teachers in Sweden (Harald Eklund), 1978.

29. The Evaluation of INSET for Teachers in Denmark (Jørgen Gregersen), 1978.

30. Synthesis Report: Reflecting upon Evaluation (T. Fox), 1980.

The utilisation of new materials

31. Synthesis Report (P. Döbrich et al.), 1980.

The role and training of teacher trainers

32. Synthesis Report (B. Mulford), 1980.

The cost and efficient utilisation of resources

33. In England and Wales (H.W. Bradley), 1978.

34. The Australian Experience (Peter Cameron), 1978.

35. Some United States Experiences (John C. Thurber), 1979.

36. A Danish Case Study (Henning Andersen and Tom Ploug Olsen), 1979.

37. The Swedish Example (S.E. Henricson), 1980.

38. Synthesis Report (P. Kaplan), 1980.

Co-development activities

39. Final conclusions of the Stockholm Conference, 1977.

40. General Report and Conclusions of the Palm Beach Workshop, 1978.

41. General Report and Conclusions of the Bournemouth Workshop, 1978.

42. International Seminar on Teacher Participation in School-Focused INSET, 1979.

43. Synthesis Report: Co-development in INSET - An Evaluation (E.S. Henderson), 1981.

B. <u>GENERAL REFERENCES</u>

The continuing interest in and commitment to INSET is evident from the burgeoning literature on the subject. In a stimulating account of European developments, Taylor spoke of "the chorus of support for improved in-service education and training for teachers that has characterised educational discussion in most developed countries in recent years" (p. 198) while related European trends are reflected in a review of EEC work by Belbenoit and in the recent emphasis on the training of administrators (McHugh and Parkes).

In a book devoted mainly to innovations in initial teacher education, Turnery reviewed INSET developments in Australia and predicted (p. 70) a steady growth in INSET over the next 25 years. In New Zealand a national review has recommended that induction and in-service should be improved (Hill).

The continuing interest in Canada is indicated in Wideen et al. (1979). Of the many publications in the United States the following are notable: an extremely thorough and comprehensive conceptual analysis by Joyce et al. (1976); a general review of the field by Rubin (1978); the newsletters and literature surveys by the National Council of States on In-Service Education (1979) and Johnson (1980) and a review of research and development priorities in teacher education carried out under the auspices of the National Institute of Education (Hall, 1979).

Relevant work in non-OECD and third world countries is discussed by Laderrière (1975), by Goble and Porter (1977), in contributions to Hoyle (1980) and in a review of progress in Anglophone Africa by Greenland et al. (1981).

This selective bibliography consists mainly of British and American studies because of the writer's familiarity with these sources. It is, of course, recognised that comparable work exists in other Member countries.

44. American Association of Colleges for Teacher Education, 1978, <u>Emerging Professional Roles for Teacher Educators</u>. Washington DC: AACTE.

45. Baker K., 1979, "The staff tutor role: a case study" in Bolam, Baker and McMahon (55).

46. Baker K., 1980, *The Schools and In-Service Teacher Education (SITE) Project: A Report on the First Year, 1978-79*, University of Bristol School of Education.

47. Batten M., 1979, *National Evaluation of the Department Program*, Canberra: Schools Commission.

48. Belbenoit G., 1979, *INSET in the European Community*, Education Series 8. Brussels: Office for Official Publications of the European Community.

49. Billings D.E., 1977, "The nature and scope of staff development in institutions of higher education" in Elton L. and Simmonds K.(eds), *Staff Development in Higher Education*, London: Society for Research into Higher Education.

50. Birdsall L., Gordon D.W. and Bond L.G., 1978. *A Framework for Building Effective, Comprehensive School Improvement and Staff Development Programs: A Process Model*, Sacramento: California State Department of Education.

51. Bolam R., 1975, "The management of educational change: Towards a conceptual framework", in Houghton V.P., McHugh C.A.R. and Morgan C.(eds.). *Management in Education Reader 1: The Management of Organisations and Individuals*, London: Ward Lock.

52. Bolam R., 1976, "The types of environment most likely to favour the active and effective participation of teachers in educational innovation" in *New Patterns of Teacher Education and Tasks - Teachers as Innovators*, Paris, OECD.

53. Bolam R., 1979, "Evaluating in-service education and training: A national perspective", *British Journal of Teacher Education*, 5.1. 1-15.

54. Bolam R. (forthcoming), *Strategies for School Improvement in the 1980s*, Paris, OECD.

55. Bolam R., Baker K. and McMahon A., 1979, "Teacher Induction Pilot Schemes: Final National Evaluation Report", University of Bristol School of Education (mimeo).

56. Bolam R., Smith G. and Canter H., 1978, *LEA Advisers and the Mechanisms of Innovation*, Windsor, Berks.: NFER.

57. Broudy H., 1979, "Options for teacher education" in Nitzke D. (ed.), *Alternative Images of the Future: Scenarios for Education and the Preparation of Teachers*, University of North Iowa, College of Education.

58. Centre for Educational Research and Innovation, 1978, *Creativity of the School: Final Report*, Paris, OECD.

59. Chambers J., 1979, "In-service training and the needs of teachers" in Porter (12).

60. Cruikshank D.R., Lorish C. and Thompson L., 1979, "What we think we know about in-service education", *Journal of Teacher Education*, 30.1. 27-32.

61. Department of Education and Science, 1972, *Teacher Education and Training*, London: HMSO.

62. Department of Education and Science, 1978 (a), *Primary Education in England*, London: HMSO.

63. Department of Education and Science, 1978 (b), *Statistics Bulletin 78: Induction and In-Service Training of Teachers* (1978 Survey), London: DES.

64. Department of Education and Science, 1978 (c), *Making INSET Work*, London: DES.

65. Drummond W.H., 1978, "Emerging roles of the college-based teacher educator" in American Association of Colleges for Teacher Education (44).

66. Ekholm M., 1978, "The School Leader Education Project - evaluation strategies" in Eklund (28).

67. Elliott J., 1979, "How do teachers learn?" in Porter (12).

68. Eraut M., 1978, "Some perspectives on consultancy in in-service education", *British Journal of In-service Education*, 4. 1/2. 95-99.

69. Feiman-Nemser S. and Floden R.E., 1979, *What's all this talk about teacher development?* Michigan State University, College of Education, Institute for Research on Teaching.

70. Fullan M., Miles M. and Taylor G., 1978, *O.D. in Schools: The State of the Art: Volume 1* (available from M. Fullan, Ontario Institute for Studies in Education, Toronto, Canada).

71. Fuller F., 1970, *Personalised education for teachers: one application of the teacher concerns model*, University of Texas, Austin, Research and Development Center for Teacher Education.

72. Getzels J.W. and Guba E.G. 1957, "Social behaviour and the administrative process". *School Review*, 65, Winter, pp. 423-441.

73. Goble N.M. and Porter J., 1977, *The Changing Role of the Teacher: International Perspectives*, Paris: UNESCO.

74. Greenfield T.B., 1975, "Theory about organisation: a new perspective and its implications for schools" in Hughes M.G. (ed.) *Administering Education: International Challenge*, London: Athlone Press.

75. Greenfield T.B., 1979, "Research in educational administration in the United States and Canada: an overview and a critique in *Educational Administration* 8.1. 207-245.

76. Greenland J. et al., 1981, *INSET in Anglophone Africa*, University of Bristol, School of Education.

77. Hall G.E., 1979, *A National Agenda for Research and Development in Teacher Education 1979-84.* The University of Texas at Austin, Research and Development Center for Teacher Education.

78. Havelock R.G., 1969, *Planning for Innovation through Dissemination and Utilization of Knowledge*, Ann Arbor, Michigan: Center for Research on Utilization of Scientific Knowledge, Institute for Social Research.

79. Henderson E., 1978(a), "The Evaluation of an Open University Course" in McCabe (27).

80. Henderson E., 1978(b), *The Evaluation of In-Service Teacher Training*, London: Croom Helm.

81. Henderson E., 1979, "The Concept of School-focused In-service Education and Training", *British Journal of Teacher Education*, 51.1. 17-25.

82. Hill C.G.N., 1979, *Review of Teacher Training*, Wellington, New Zealand: Department of Education.

83. Hite H. and McIntyre P., 1978, *Planning In-Service Education*, Bellingham, Washington: Western Washington University.

84. Houston W.R., 1978, "Emerging roles of the school-based teacher educator", AACTE (44).

85. Howey K., 1976, "Cultural perspectives and evolving trends in in-service education in the United States" in Rubin and Howey (108).

86. Hoyle E.(ed), 1981, *World Yearbook of Education 1980: The Professional Development of Teachers*, London: Kogan Page.

87. Jenkins W.I., 1978, *Policy Analysis*, London: Martin Robertson.

88. Johnson M., 1980. *Professional Development: In-service Education: Priority for the 1980s*. Syracuse University School of Education: National Council of States on In-service Education.

89. Joyce B.R. (ed.), 1978, *Involvement: A Study of Shared Governance of Teacher Education*, New York: Syracuse University.

90. Joyce B.R., Howey K.R., Yarger S.J., Hill W.C., Waterman F.T., Vance B.A., Parker D.W. and Baker M.G., 1976, *In-service Teacher Education, Report 1: Issues to Face*, New York: Syracuse University, National Dissemination Center.

91. Joyce B.R. and Showers B., 1980, "Improving in-service training: the messages of research" in *Educational Leadership*, February, 379-385.

92. Katz L.G., 1974, "The advisory approach to in-service training", *Journal of Teacher Education* 25.2. 154-159.

93. Kogan M., 1980. The Dutch Support System in an International Perspective in Educational Support Systems: the Netherlands debate, Paris: OECD/CERI.

94. Laderrière P., 1975, *Trends and Innovations in Teacher Education: Educational Documentation and Information Bulletin No. 195*, Paris: UNESCO, International Bureau of Education.

95. Larsson T., 1978, "The 'Local School Development Planning and Evaluation' Project" in Eklund (28).

96. Lawrence G., et al., 1974, *Patterns of Effective In-Service Education*, Tallahassee, Florida: Department of Education.

97. Lawrence G. and Branch J., 1978, "Peer support system as the heart of in-service education", *Theory into Practice*, 17.3. 245-247.

98. McHugh R. and Parker D., 1979, "Editorial", *Educational Administration*, 7.1, i-iv.

99. McLaughlin M.W. and Marsh D., 1978, "Staff development and school change", *Teachers College Record*, 80.1. 69-94.

100. McMahon A., 1979, "The external tutor role: three case studies" in Bolam, Baker and McMahon (55).

101. National Council of States on In-service Education, 1979(a), <u>Professional Development: Sources and Resources: an Annotated Bibliography on In-Service Education</u>, Syracuse University, School of Education.

102. National Council of States on In-service Education, 1979(b), <u>In-Service: January Issue</u>, Syracuse University, School of Education.

103. Nicholson A.M., Joyce B.R., Parker D.W. and Waterman F.E., 1977, <u>The Literature on In-Service Teacher Education: An Analytic Review</u>, The National Dissemination Center, Syracuse University, 123 Huntington Hall, Syracuse, New York 13210.

104. Olsen T.P., 1978, "The Lundebjerg Project: a study of school based INSET" in Gregersen (29).

105. Perry P., 1977, <u>Final Conclusions of the Stockholm Conference on Strategies for School-focused Support Structure for Teachers in Change and Innovation</u>, Paris, OECD.

106. Pickford M., 1975, <u>University Expansion and Finance</u>, London: Chatto and Windus Ltd., for Sussex University Press.

107. Rauh P.S., 1978, "Helping teacher: A model for staff development", <u>Teachers' College Record</u>, 80.1. 172-187.

108. Rubin L. and Howey K., 1976, <u>Innovation in INSET: United States</u>, Paris, OECD.

109. Rubin L. (ed.), 1978, <u>The In-Service Education of Teachers</u>, London: Allyn and Bacon Inc.

110. Schmuck R.A., 1974, "Interventions for strengthening the school's creativity" in Nisbet J (ed.), <u>Creativity of the School</u>, Paris, OECD.

111. Stake R., 1976, <u>Evaluating Educational Programmes: The Need and the Response</u>, Paris, OECD.

112. Steadman S., 1976, "Techniques of Evaluation" in Tawney D. (ed.), <u>Curriculum Evaluation Today: Trends and Implications</u>, London, MacMillan.

113. Taylor W., 1978, <u>Research and Reform in Teacher Education</u>, Windsor, Berkshire: National Foundation for Education Research Publishing Company.

114. Taylor W., 1980, Untitled paper (mimeo), University of London, Institute of Education.

115. Turney C., (ed.), 1977, *Innovation in Teacher Education*, Sydney: Sydney University Press.

116. van Velzen W. (ed.), 1979, *Developing an Autonomous School*, The Hague: Dutch Catholic School Council.

117. Westoby A., 1976, *Costs in Education: University Examples Unit 8, Open University Course E321, Management in Education*, Bletchley: Open University Press.

118. Wideen M., Hopkins D. and Pye I. (eds.), 1979, *In-Service: A Means of Progress in Tough Times*, Faculty of Education, Simon Fraser University, Vancouver, British Columbia.

119. World Confederation of Organisations of the Teaching Profession, 1980. *Views Submitted to the Conference on INSET and Strategies for Educational Change*. Paris, OECD/CERI.

120. Yarger S.J. and Galluzzo G.R., 1980. "Grabbing at Mirages or Painting Clear Pictures?... Toward Solving the Dilemmas of Research on In-service Teacher Education" (mimeo), Syracuse University.

OECD SALES AGENTS
DÉPOSITAIRES DES PUBLICATIONS DE L'OCDE

ARGENTINA – ARGENTINE
Carlos Hirsch S.R.L., Florida 165, 4° Piso (Galería Guemes)
1333 BUENOS AIRES, Tel. 33.1787.2391 y 30.7122
AUSTRALIA – AUSTRALIE
Australia and New Zealand Book Company Pty, Ltd.,
10 Aquatic Drive, Frenchs Forest, N.S.W. 2086
P.O. Box 459, BROOKVALE, N.S.W. 2100
AUSTRIA – AUTRICHE
OECD Publications and Information Center
4 Simrockstrasse 5300 BONN. Tel. (0228) 21.60.45
Local Agent/Agent local :
Gerold and Co., Graben 31, WIEN 1. Tel. 52.22.35
BELGIUM – BELGIQUE
CCLS – LCLS
19, rue Plantin, 1070 BRUXELLES. Tel. 02.512.89.74
BRAZIL – BRÉSIL
Mestre Jou S.A., Rua Guaipa 518,
Caixa Postal 24090, 05089 SAO PAULO 10. Tel. 261.1920
Rua Senador Dantas 19 s/205-6, RIO DE JANEIRO GB.
Tel. 232.07.32
CANADA
Renouf Publishing Company Limited,
2182 St. Catherine Street West,
MONTRÉAL, Que. H3H 1M7. Tel. (514)937.3519
OTTAWA, Ont. K1P 5A6, 61 Sparks Street
DENMARK – DANEMARK
Munksgaard Export and Subscription Service
35, Nørre Søgade
DK 1370 KØBENHAVN K. Tel. +45.1.12.85.70
FINLAND – FINLANDE
Akateeminen Kirjakauppa
Keskuskatu 1, 00100 HELSINKI 10. Tel. 65.11.22
FRANCE
Bureau des Publications de l'OCDE,
2 rue André-Pascal, 75775 PARIS CEDEX 16. Tel. (1) 524.81.67
Principal correspondant :
13602 AIX-EN-PROVENCE : Librairie de l'Université.
Tel. 26.18.08
GERMANY – ALLEMAGNE
OECD Publications and Information Center
4 Simrockstrasse 5300 BONN Tel. (0228) 21.60.45
GREECE – GRÈCE
Librairie Kauffmann, 28 rue du Stade,
ATHÈNES 132. Tel. 322.21.60
HONG-KONG
Government Information Services,
Publications/Sales Section, Baskerville House,
2/F., 22 Ice House Street
ICELAND – ISLANDE
Snaebjörn Jönsson and Co., h.f.,
Hafnarstraeti 4 and 9, P.O.B. 1131, REYKJAVIK.
Tel. 13133/14281/11936
INDIA – INDE
Oxford Book and Stationery Co. :
NEW DELHI-1, Scindia House. Tel. 45896
CALCUTTA 700016, 17 Park Street. Tel. 240832
INDONESIA – INDONÉSIE
PDIN-LIPI, P.O. Box 3065/JKT., JAKARTA, Tel. 583467
IRELAND – IRLANDE
TDC Publishers – Library Suppliers
12 North Frederick Street, DUBLIN 1 Tel. 744835-749677
ITALY – ITALIE
Libreria Commissionaria Sansoni :
Via Lamarmora 45, 50121 FIRENZE. Tel. 579751/584468
Via Bartolini 29, 20155 MILANO. Tel. 365083
Sub-depositari :
Ugo Tassi
Via A. Farnese 28, 00192 ROMA. Tel. 310590
Editrice e Libreria Herder,
Piazza Montecitorio 120, 00186 ROMA. Tel. 6794628
Costantino Ercolano, Via Generale Orsini 46, 80132 NAPOLI. Tel. 405210
Libreria Hoepli, Via Hoepli 5, 20121 MILANO. Tel. 865446
Libreria Scientifica, Dott. Lucio de Biasio "Aeiou"
Via Meravigli 16, 20123 MILANO. Tel. 807679
Libreria Zanichelli
Piazza Galvani 1/A, 40124 Bologna Tel. 237389
Libreria Lattes, Via Garibaldi 3, 10122 TORINO. Tel. 519274
La diffusione delle edizioni OCSE è inoltre assicurata dalle migliori librerie nelle città più importanti.
JAPAN – JAPON
OECD Publications and Information Center,
Landic Akasaka Bldg., 2-3-4 Akasaka,
Minato-ku, TOKYO 107 Tel. 586.2016
KOREA – CORÉE
Pan Korea Book Corporation,
P.O. Box n° 101 Kwangwhamun, SÉOUL. Tel. 72.7369

LEBANON – LIBAN
Documenta Scientifica/Redico,
Edison Building, Bliss Street, P.O. Box 5641, BEIRUT.
Tel. 354429 – 344425
MALAYSIA – MALAISIE
and/et **SINGAPORE – SINGAPOUR**
University of Malaya Co-operative Bookshop Ltd.
P.O. Box 1127, Jalan Pantai Baru
KUALA LUMPUR. Tel. 51425, 54058, 54361
THE NETHERLANDS – PAYS-BAS
Staatsuitgeverij
Verzendboekhandel Chr. Plantijnstraat 1
Postbus 20014
2500 EA S-GRAVENHAGE. Tel. nr. 070.789911
Voor bestellingen: Tel. 070.789208
NEW ZEALAND – NOUVELLE-ZÉLANDE
Publications Section,
Government Printing Office Bookshops:
AUCKLAND: Retail Bookshop: 25 Rutland Street,
Mail Orders: 85 Beach Road, Private Bag C.P.O.
HAMILTON: Retail Ward Street,
Mail Orders, P.O. Box 857
WELLINGTON: Retail: Mulgrave Street (Head Office),
Cubacade World Trade Centre
Mail Orders: Private Bag
CHRISTCHURCH: Retail: 159 Hereford Street,
Mail Orders: Private Bag
DUNEDIN: Retail: Princes Street
Mail Order: P.O. Box 1104
NORWAY – NORVÈGE
J.G. TANUM A/S Karl Johansgate 43
P.O. Box 1177 Sentrum OSLO 1. Tel. (02) 80.12.60
PAKISTAN
Mirza Book Agency, 65 Shahrah Quaid-E-Azam, LAHORE 3.
Tel. 66839
PHILIPPINES
National Book Store, Inc.
Library Services Division, P.O. Box 1934, MANILA.
Tel. Nos. 49.43.06 to 09, 40.53.45, 49.45.12
PORTUGAL
Livraria Portugal, Rua do Carmo 70-74,
1117 LISBOA CODEX. Tel. 360582/3
SPAIN – ESPAGNE
Mundi-Prensa Libros, S.A.
Castelló 37, Apartado 1223, MADRID-1. Tel. 275.46.55
Libreria Bosch, Ronda Universidad 11, BARCELONA 7.
Tel. 317.53.08, 317.53.58
SWEDEN – SUÈDE
AB CE Fritzes Kungl Hovbokhandel,
Box 16 356, S 103 27 STH, Regeringsgatan 12,
DS STOCKHOLM. Tel. 08/23.89.00
SWITZERLAND – SUISSE
OECD Publications and Information Center
4 Simrockstrasse 5300 BONN. Tel. (0228) 21.60.45
Local Agents/Agents locaux
Librairie Payot, 6 rue Grenus, 1211 GENÈVE 11. Tel. 022.31.89.50
TAIWAN – FORMOSE
Good Faith Worldwide Int'l Co., Ltd.
9th floor, No. 118, Sec. 2
Chung Hsiao E. Road
TAIPEI. Tel. 391.7396/391.7397
THAILAND – THAILANDE
Suksit Siam Co., Ltd., 1715 Rama IV Rd,
Samyan, BANGKOK 5. Tel. 2511630
TURKEY – TURQUIE
Kültur Yayinlari Is-Türk Ltd. Sti.
Atatürk Bulvari No : 77/B
KIZILAY/ANKARA. Tel. 17 02 66
Dolmabahce Cad. No : 29
BESIKTAS/ISTANBUL. Tel. 60 71 88
UNITED KINGDOM – ROYAUME-UNI
H.M. Stationery Office, P.O.B. 569,
LONDON SE1   9NH. Tel. 01.928.6977, Ext. 410 or
49 High Holborn, LONDON WC1V 6 HB (personal callers)
Branches at: EDINBURGH, BIRMINGHAM, BRISTOL,
MANCHESTER, BELFAST.
UNITED STATES OF AMERICA – ÉTATS-UNIS
OECD Publications and Information Center, Suite 1207,
1750 Pennsylvania Ave., N.W. WASHINGTON, D.C.20006 – 4582
Tel. (202) 724.1857
VENEZUELA
Libreria del Este, Avda. F. Miranda 52, Edificio Galipan,
CARACAS 106. Tel. 32.23.01/33.26.04/33.24.73
YUGOSLAVIA – YOUGOSLAVIE
Jugoslovenska Knjiga, Terazije 27, P.O.B. 36, BEOGRAD.
Tel. 621.992

Les commandes provenant de pays où l'OCDE n'a pas encore désigné de dépositaire peuvent être adressées à :
OCDE, Bureau des Publications, 2, rue André-Pascal, 75775 PARIS CEDEX 16.
Orders and inquiries from countries where sales agents have not yet been appointed may be sent to:
OECD, Publications Office, 2 rue André-Pascal, 75775 PARIS CEDEX 16.

65716-10-1982

OECD PUBLICATIONS, 2, rue André-Pascal, 75775 PARIS CEDEX 16 - No. 42355 1982
PRINTED IN FRANCE
(96 82 03 1) ISBN 92-64-12372-5